Belongs to

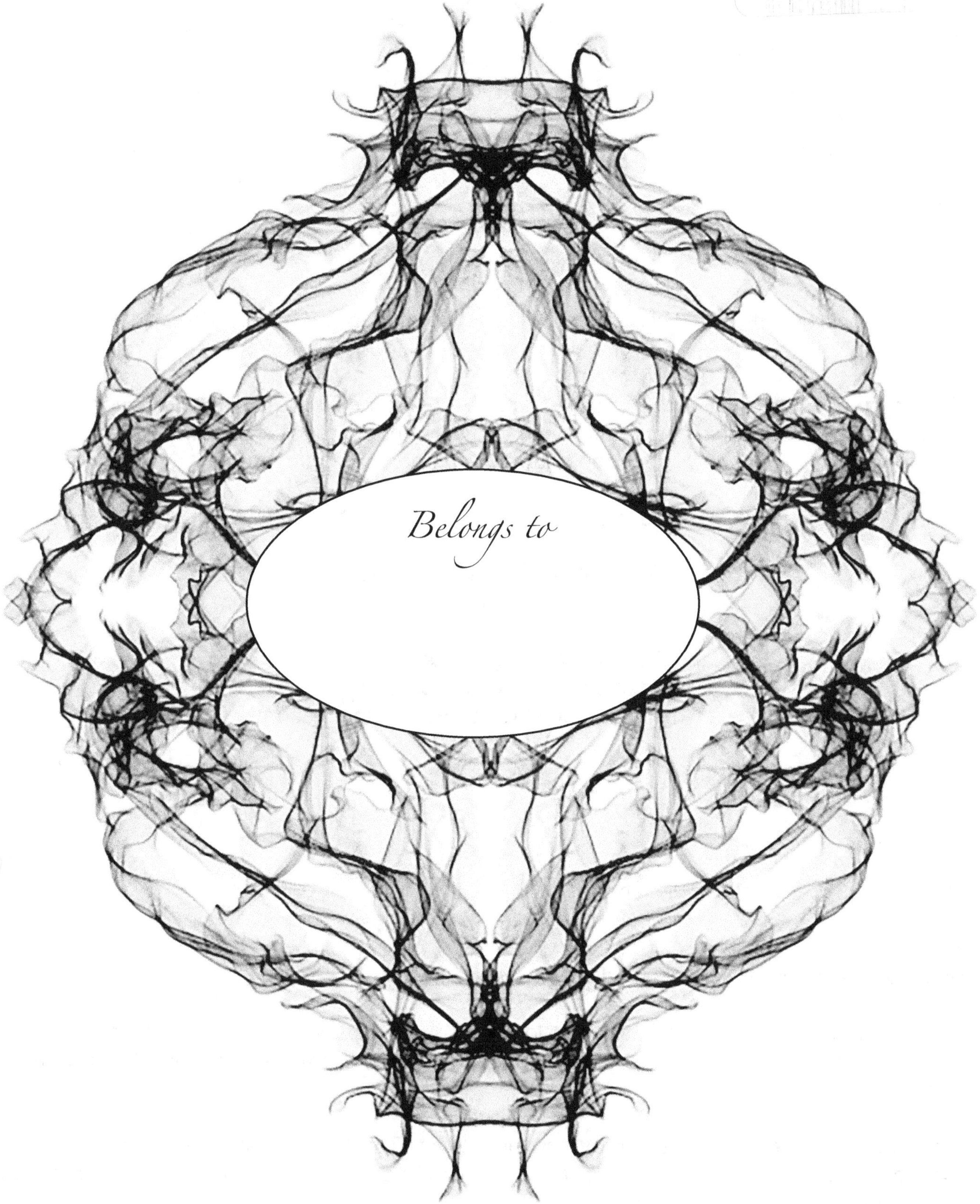

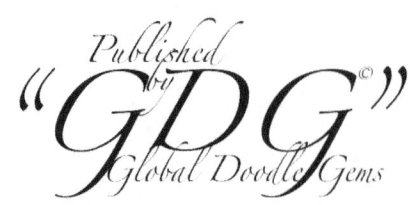

Share your colored versions with us ! We love seeing your results and hearing from you we are social !

The Official FB book page, stay on top of what we have in the works !
www.facebook.com/globaldoodlegems

The Community group, share your colored pages, meet the artists, enjoy exclusive freebies, take part in community Charity books and so much more......
www.facebook.com/groups/globaldoodlegems/

Follow us on Twitter.... @GlobalDoodlegem

We are on Instagram too
@globaldoodlegems for instagram

...and if you are not social like that we have a blog
globaldoodlegems.wordpress.com
mephistocoloringtherapy.wordpress.com

Copyright © 2016 Global Doodle Gems

All rights are reserved by Global Doodle Gems.

Duplication of pages for personal use are allowed. You are invited to color the pages then scan/post your coloured versions to social networks, mentioning the book title and author/artist (Global Doodle Gems).

All artwork and images are protected by copyright laws. This book or any portion thereof may not, otherwise, be reproduced and/or distributed or transmitted without the express written permission of the artist/publisher of Global Doodle Gems.

All of us from the Global Doodle Gems wish you a colortastic time and look forward to seeing your wonderful color results online !

Global Doodle Gems
proudly presents
"Mephisto Coloring Therapy"
The Mephisto Coloring Therapy series has been designed
to spark your imagination,
hopefully these designs will bring you lots
of hours of relaxing
coloring fun.

Cover Colored
by
Johanna Ans

Designs
by
Maria Wedel

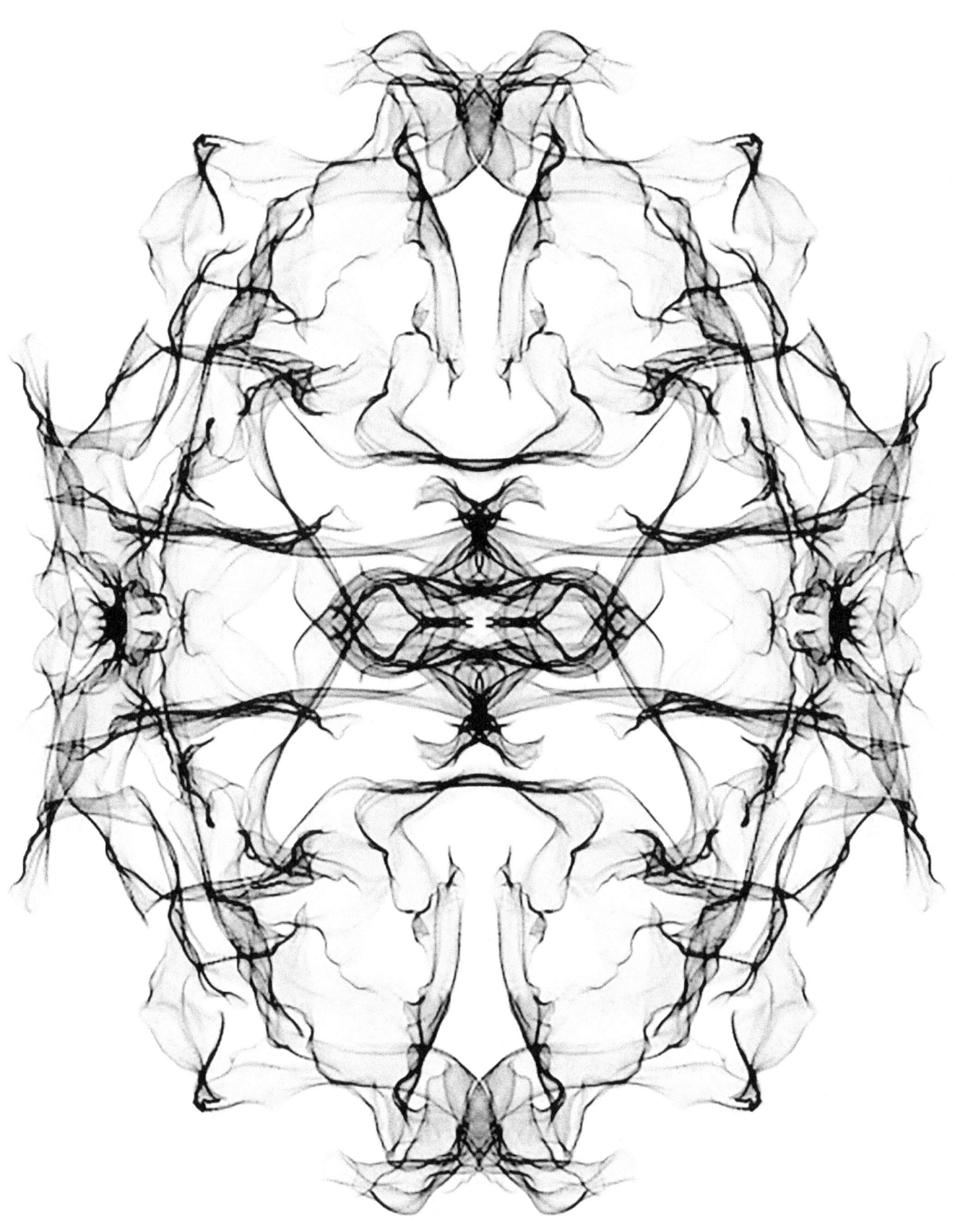

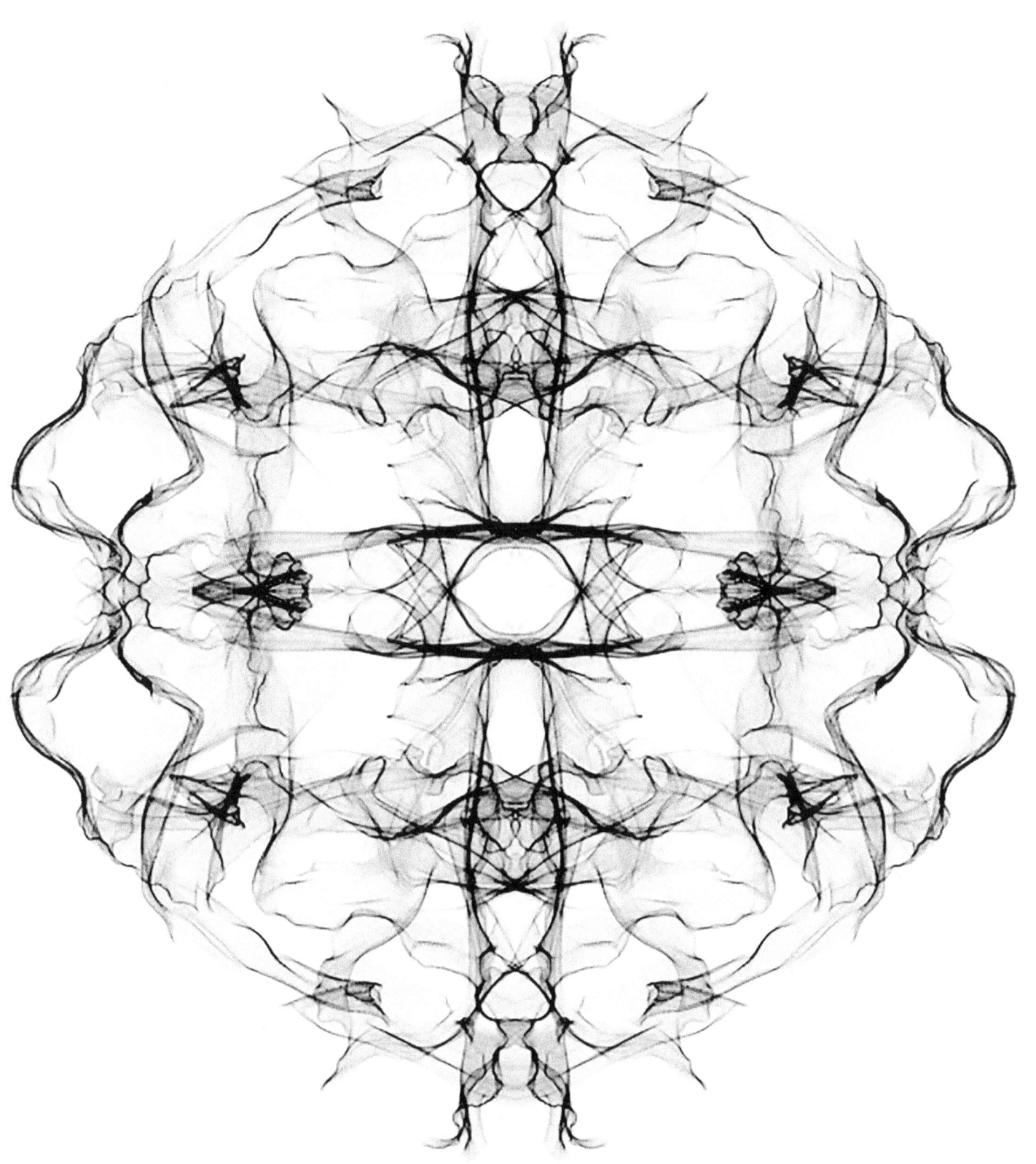

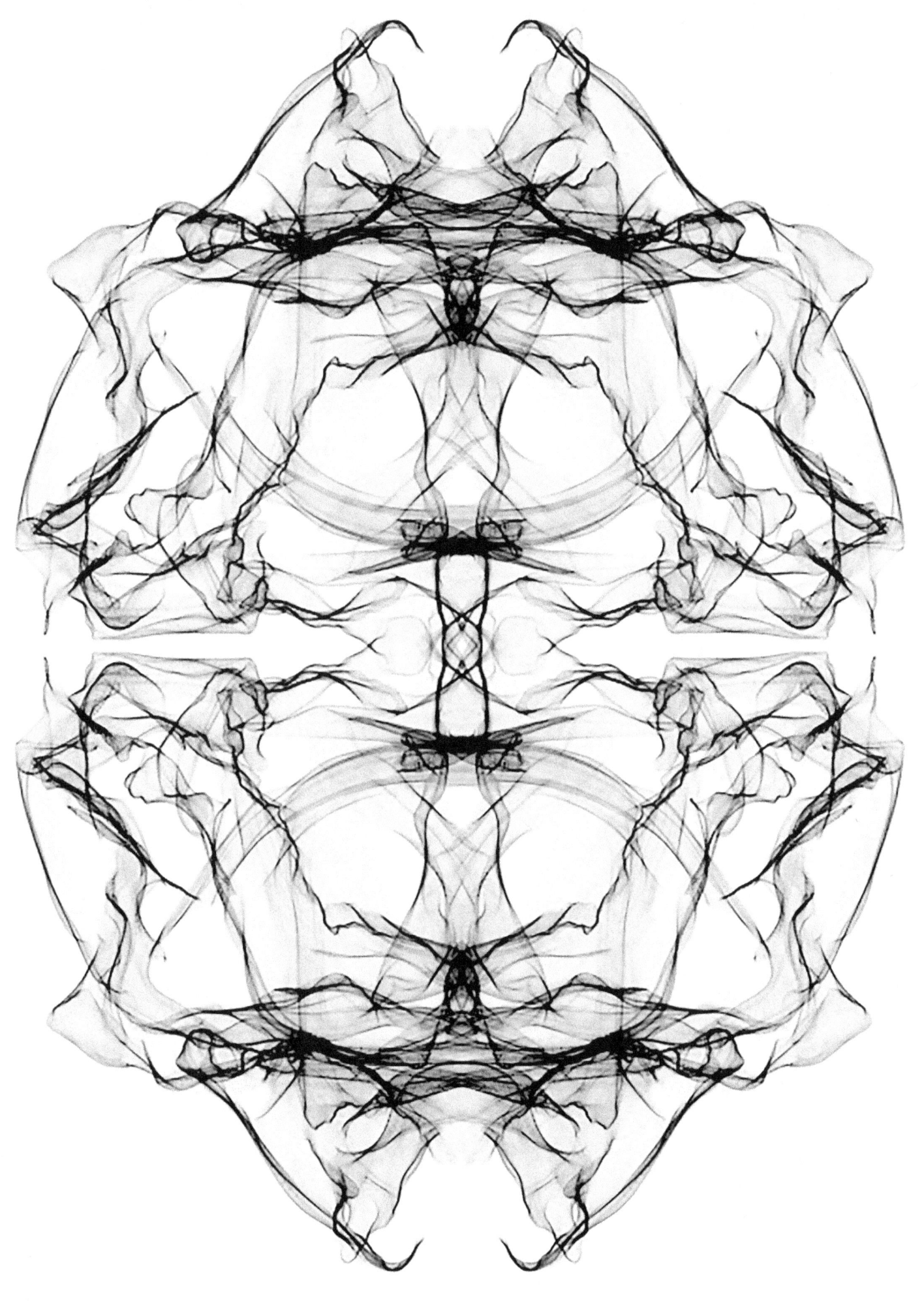

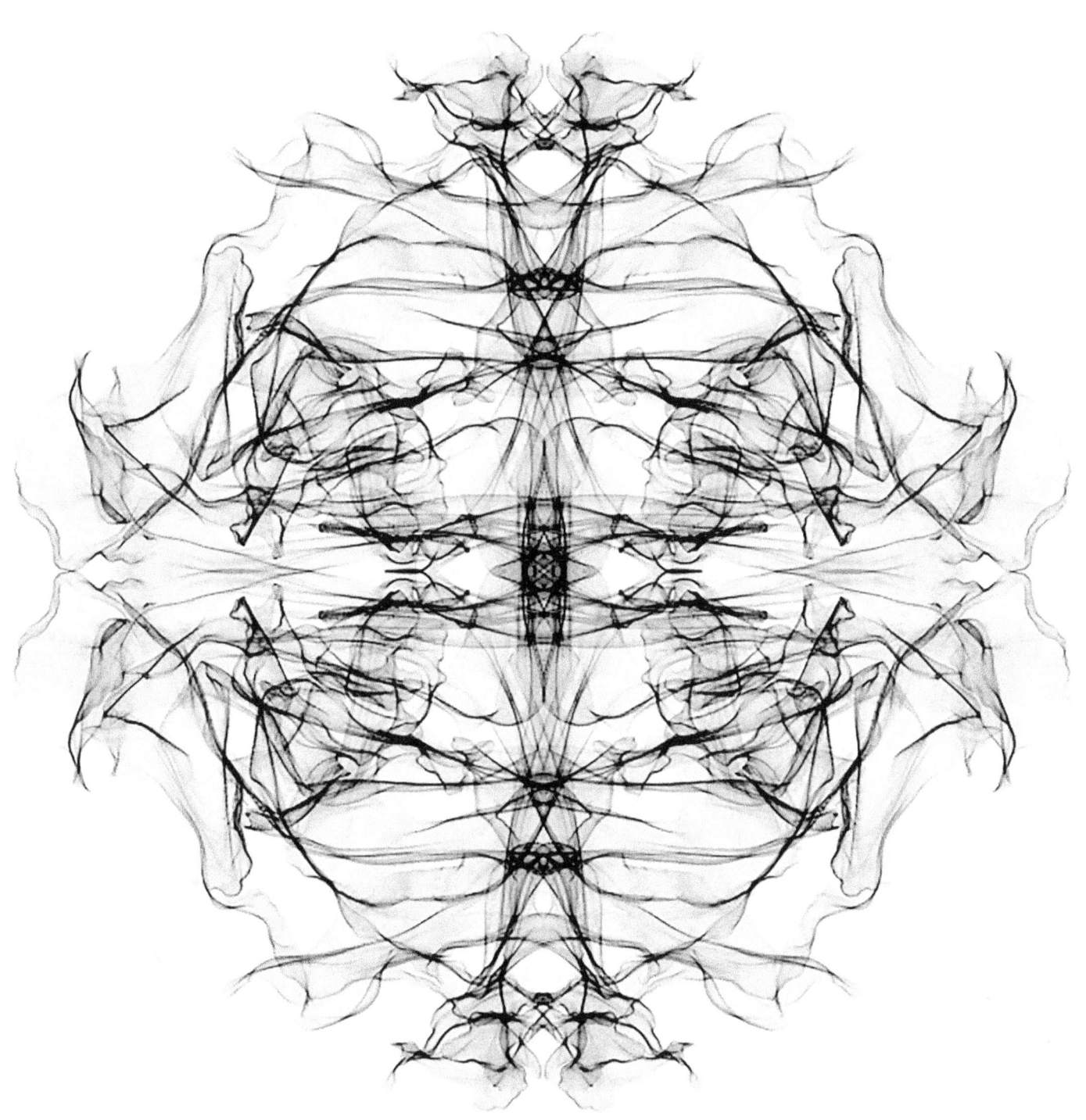

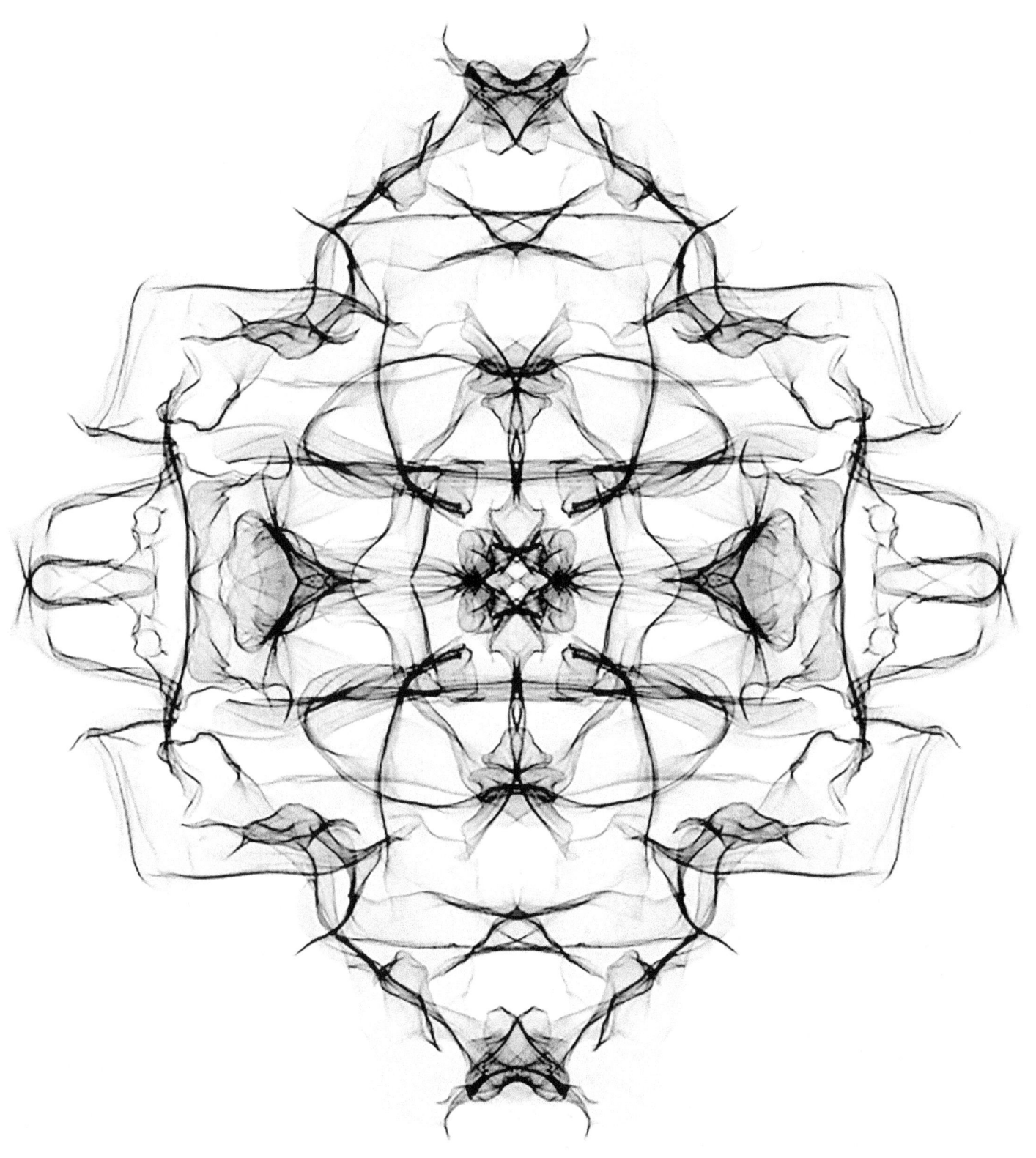

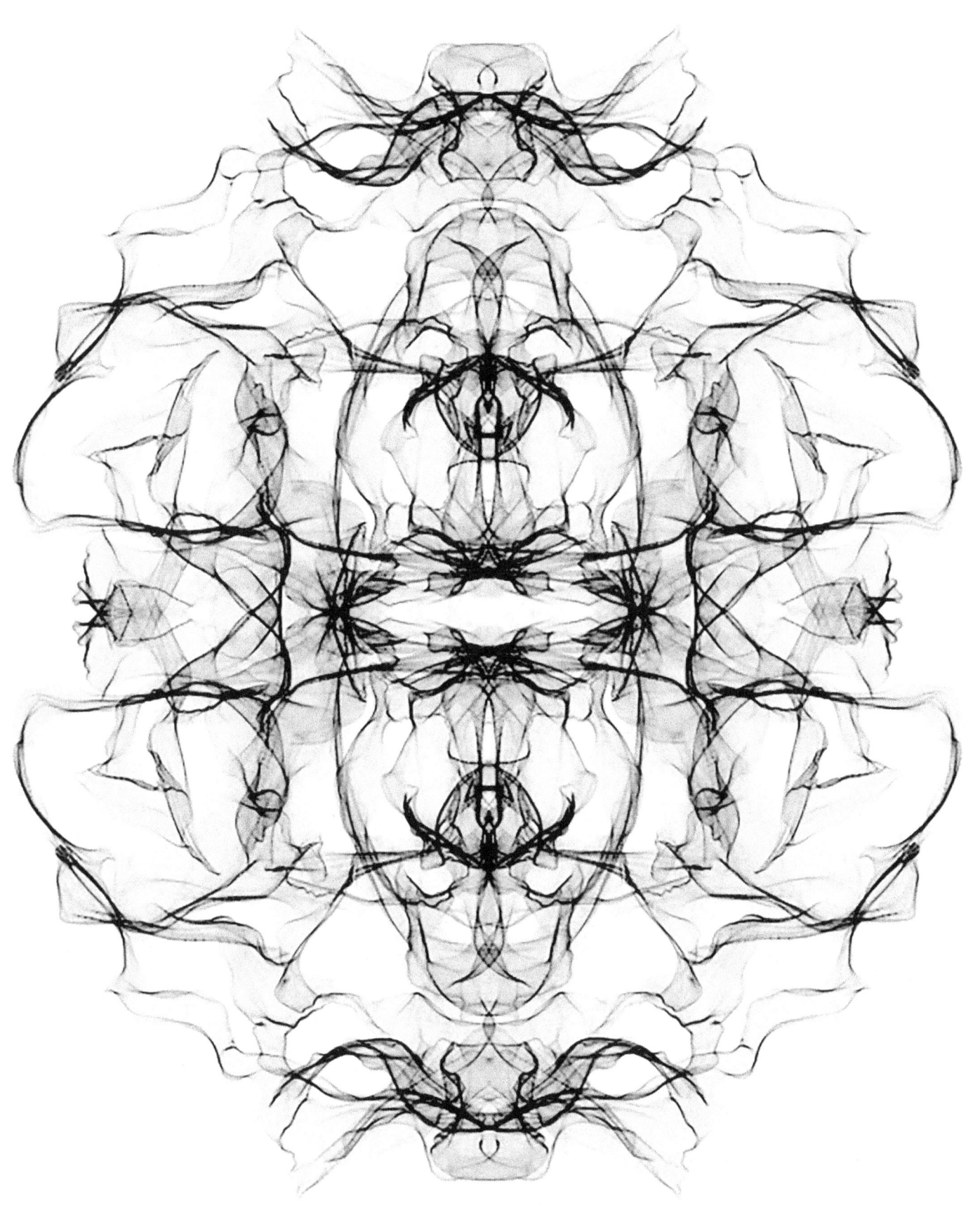

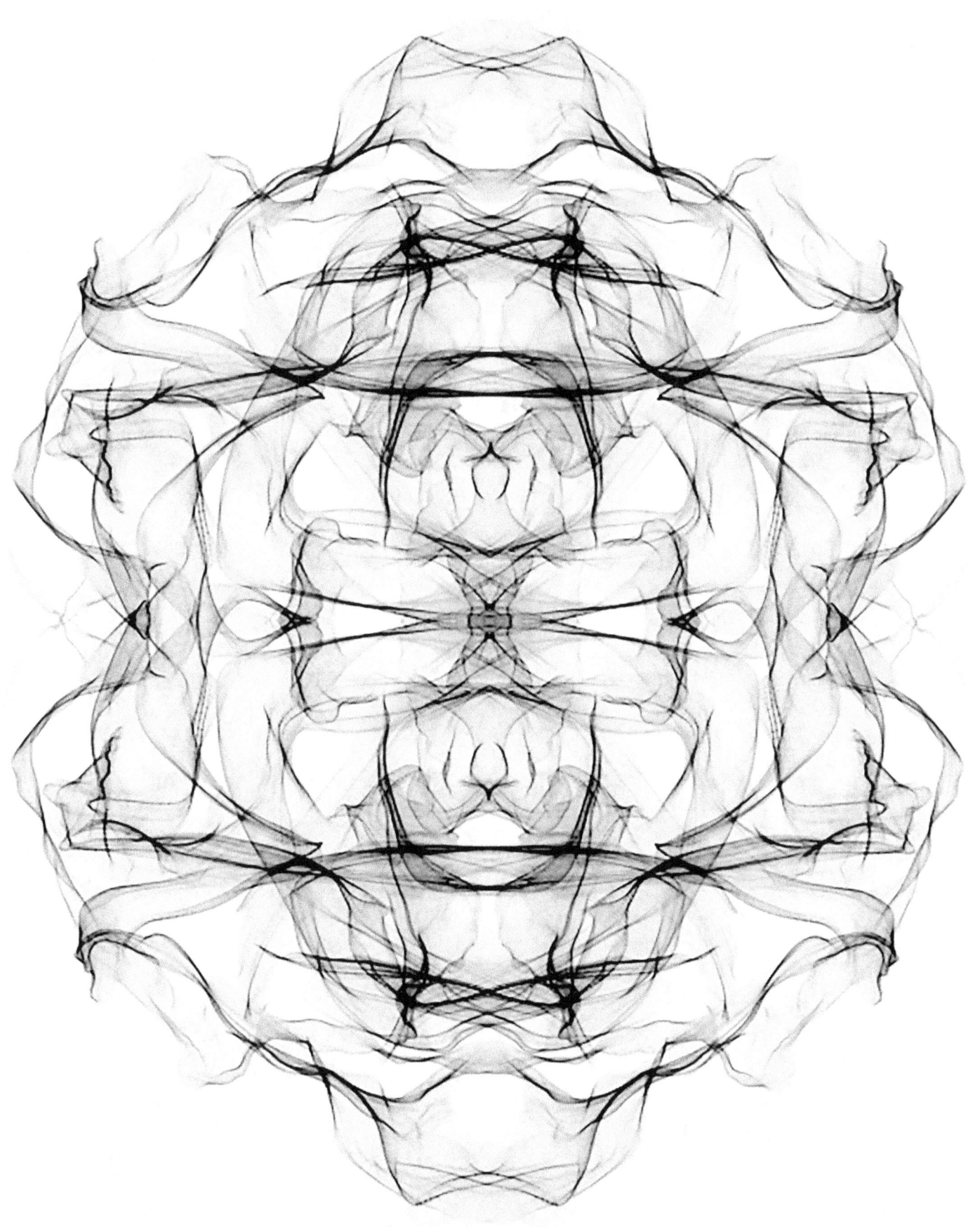

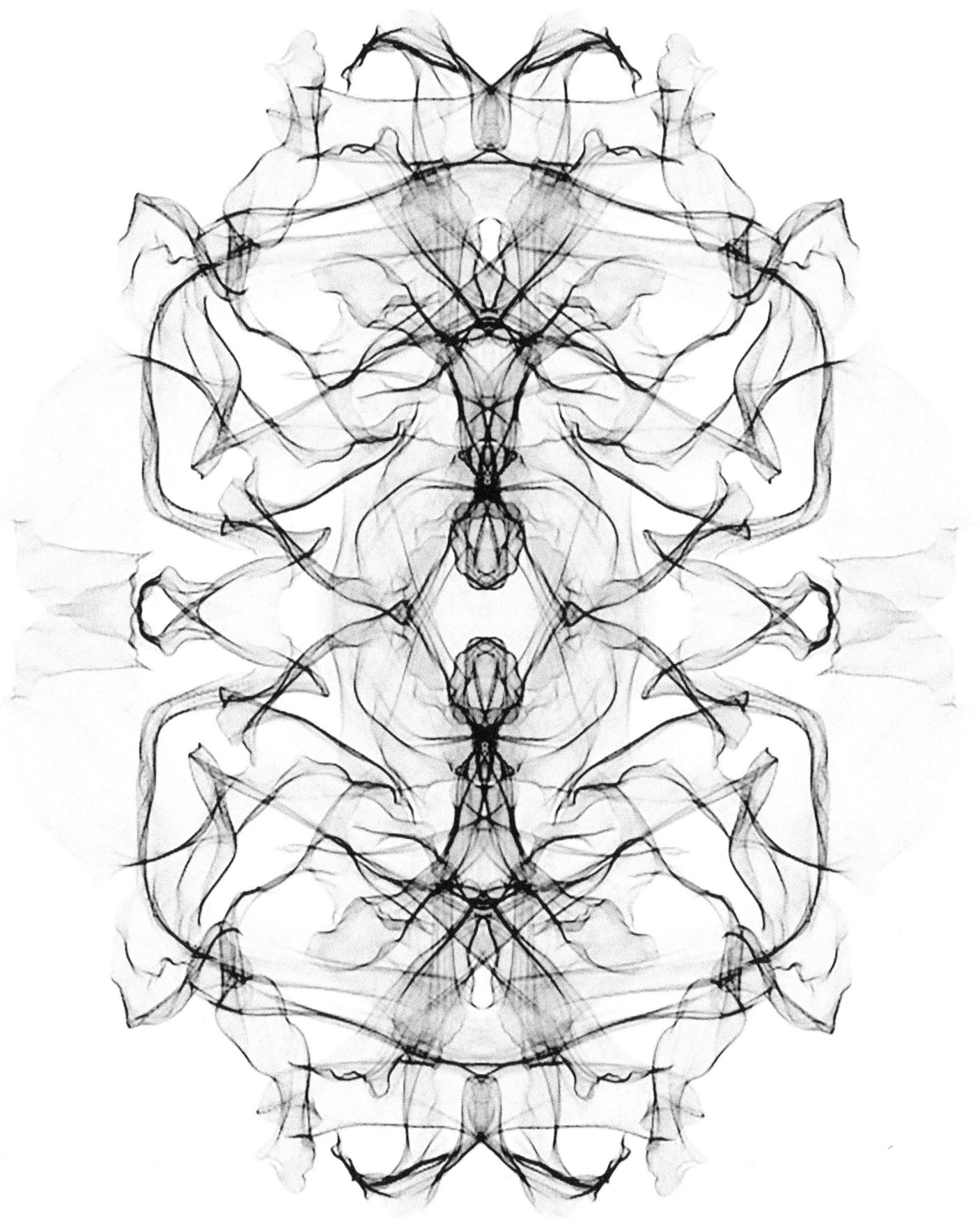

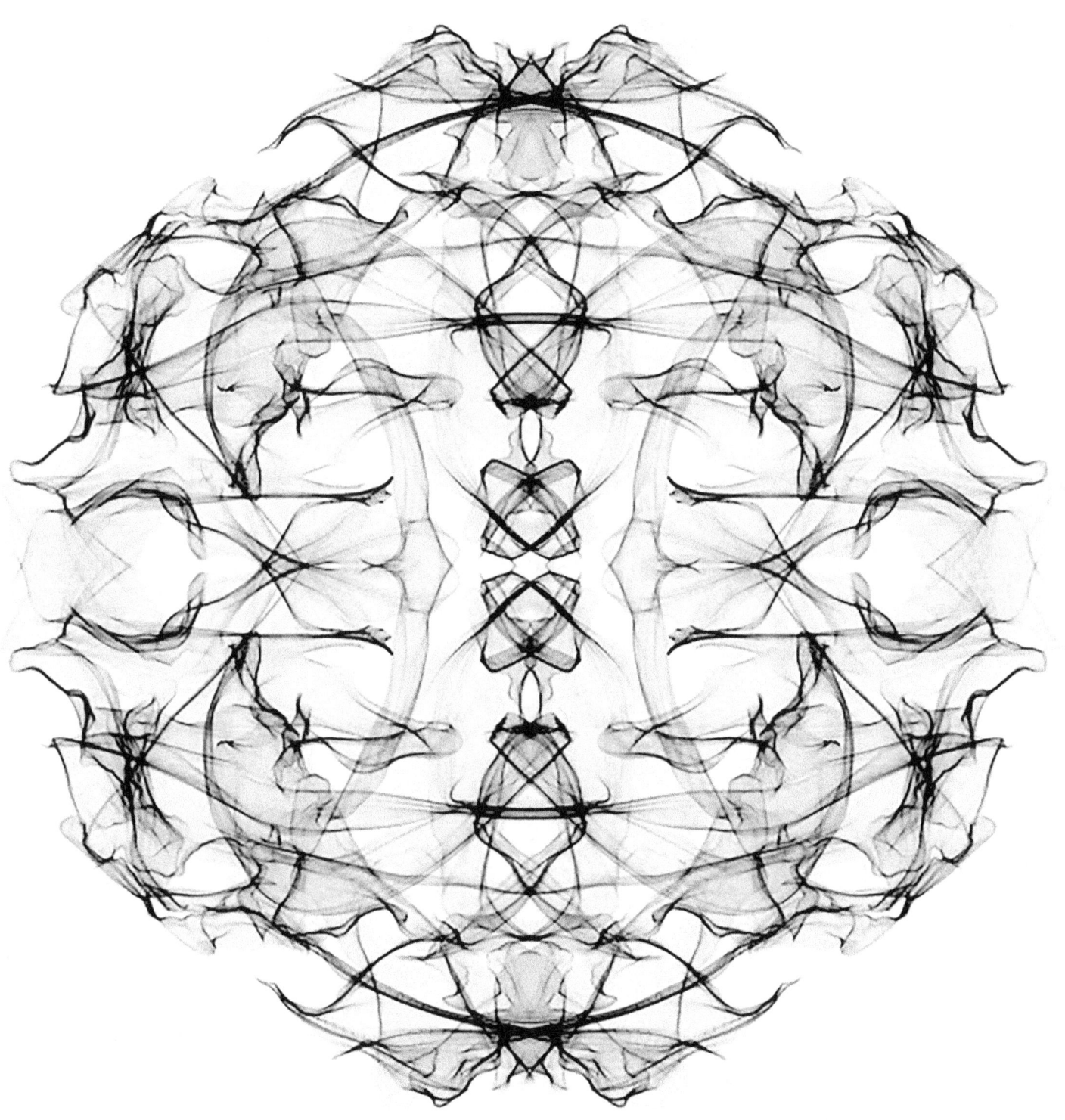

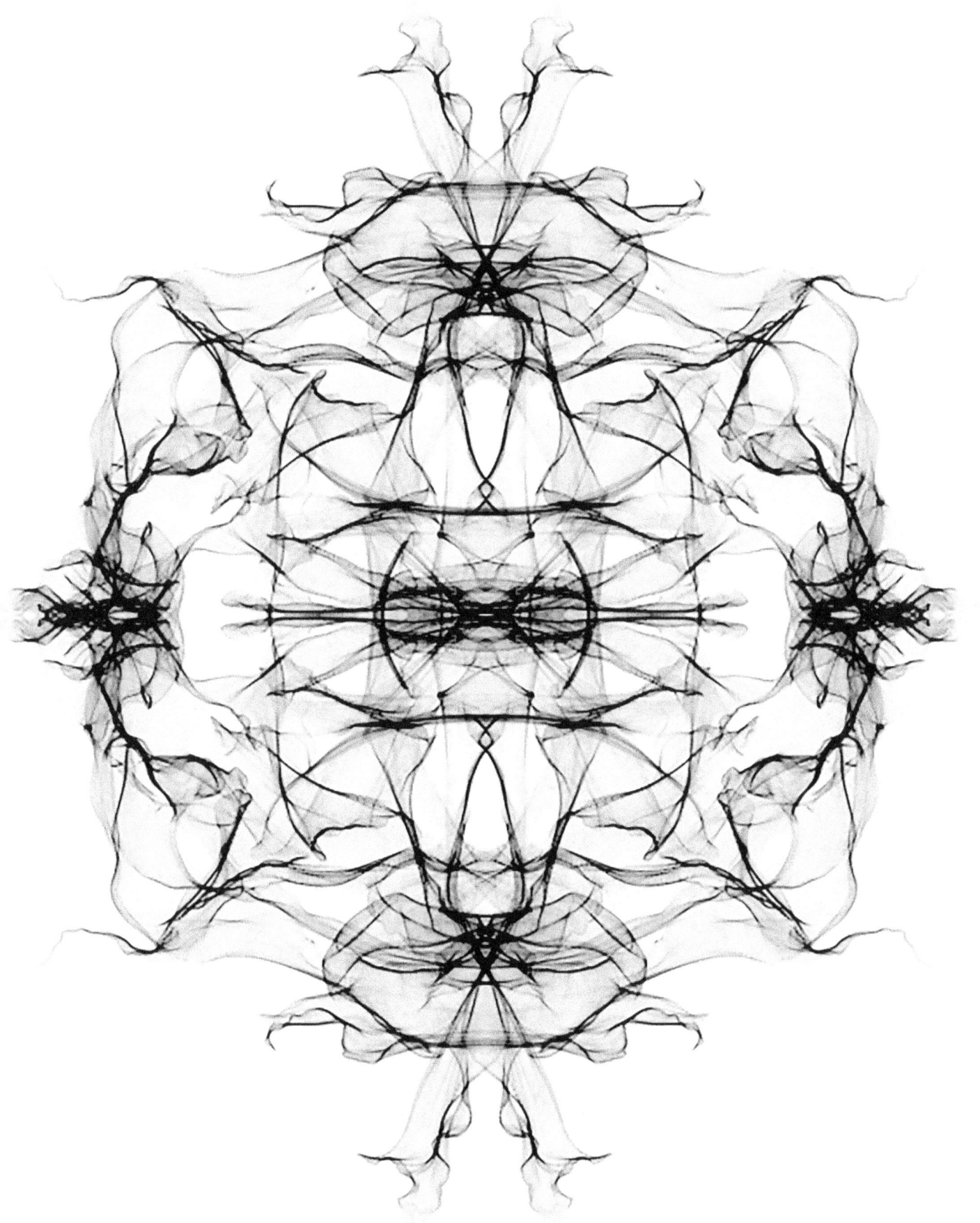

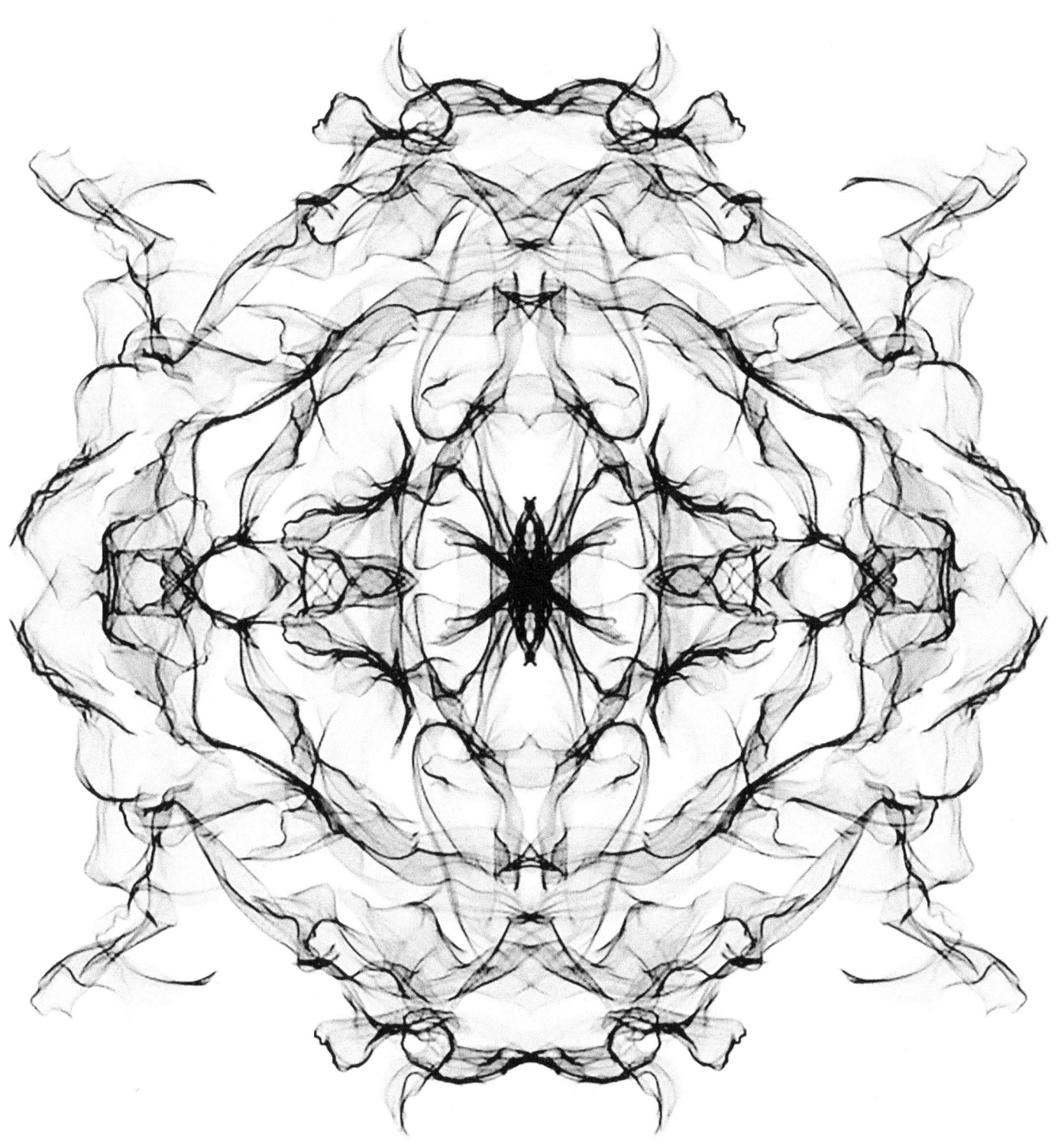

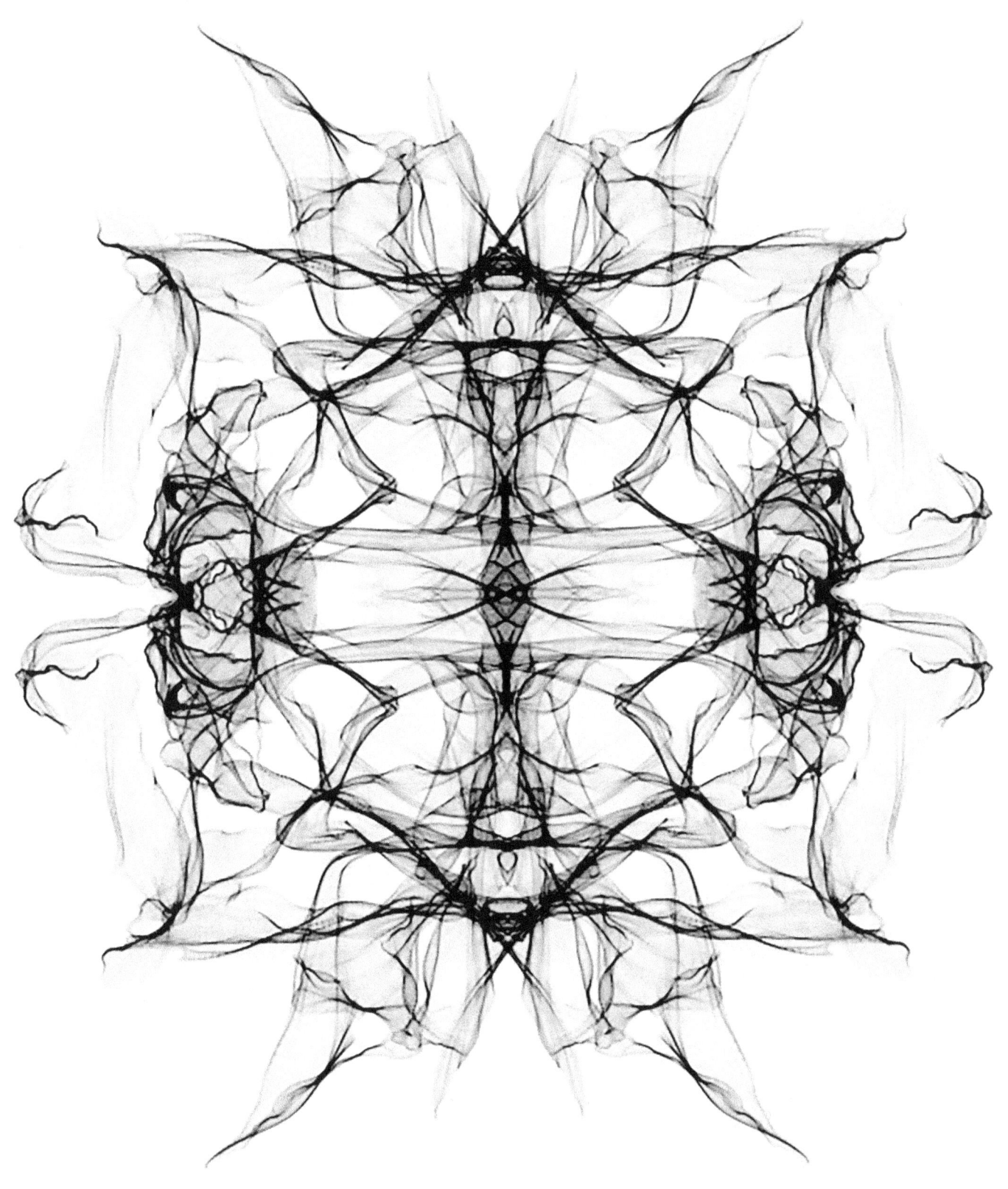

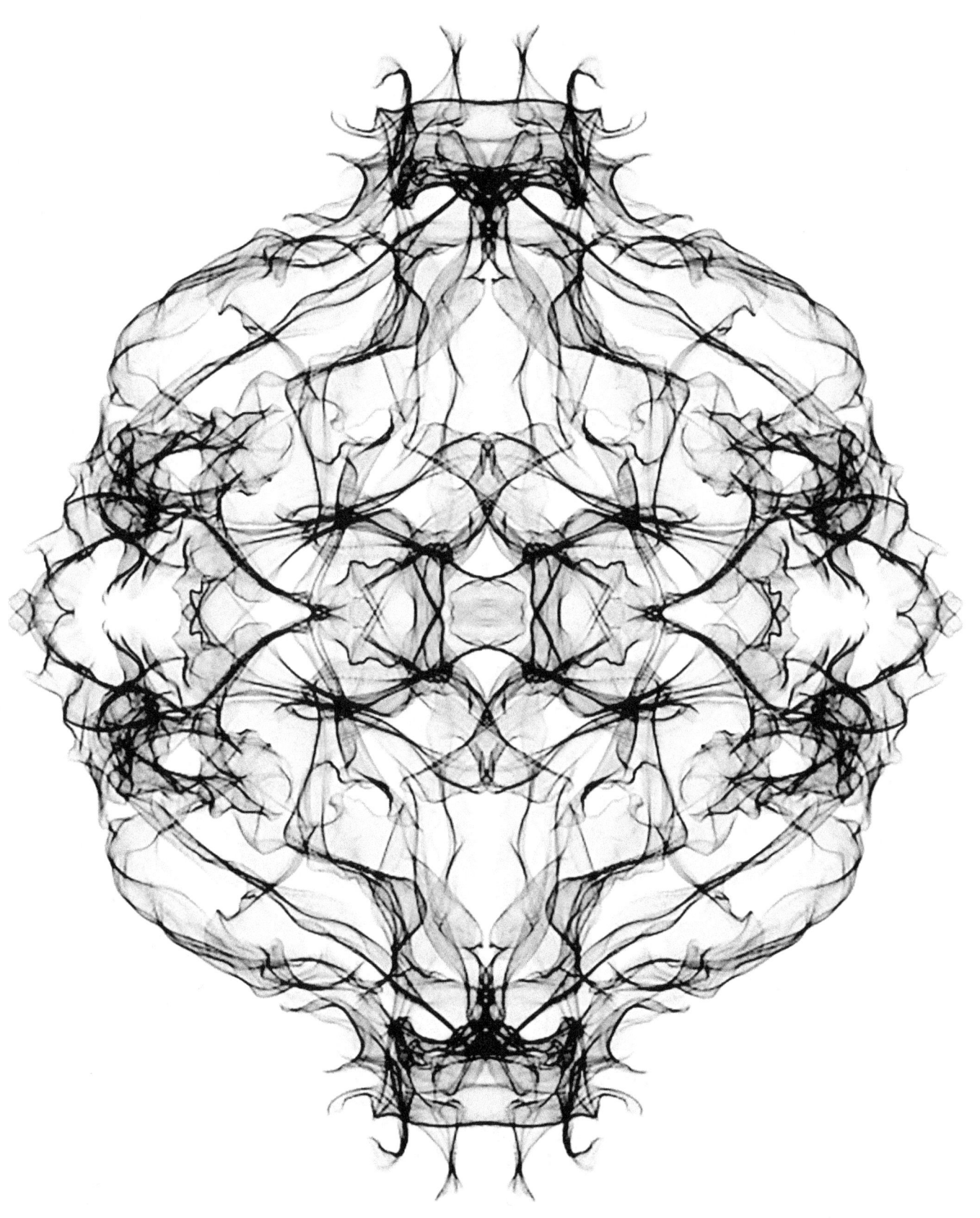

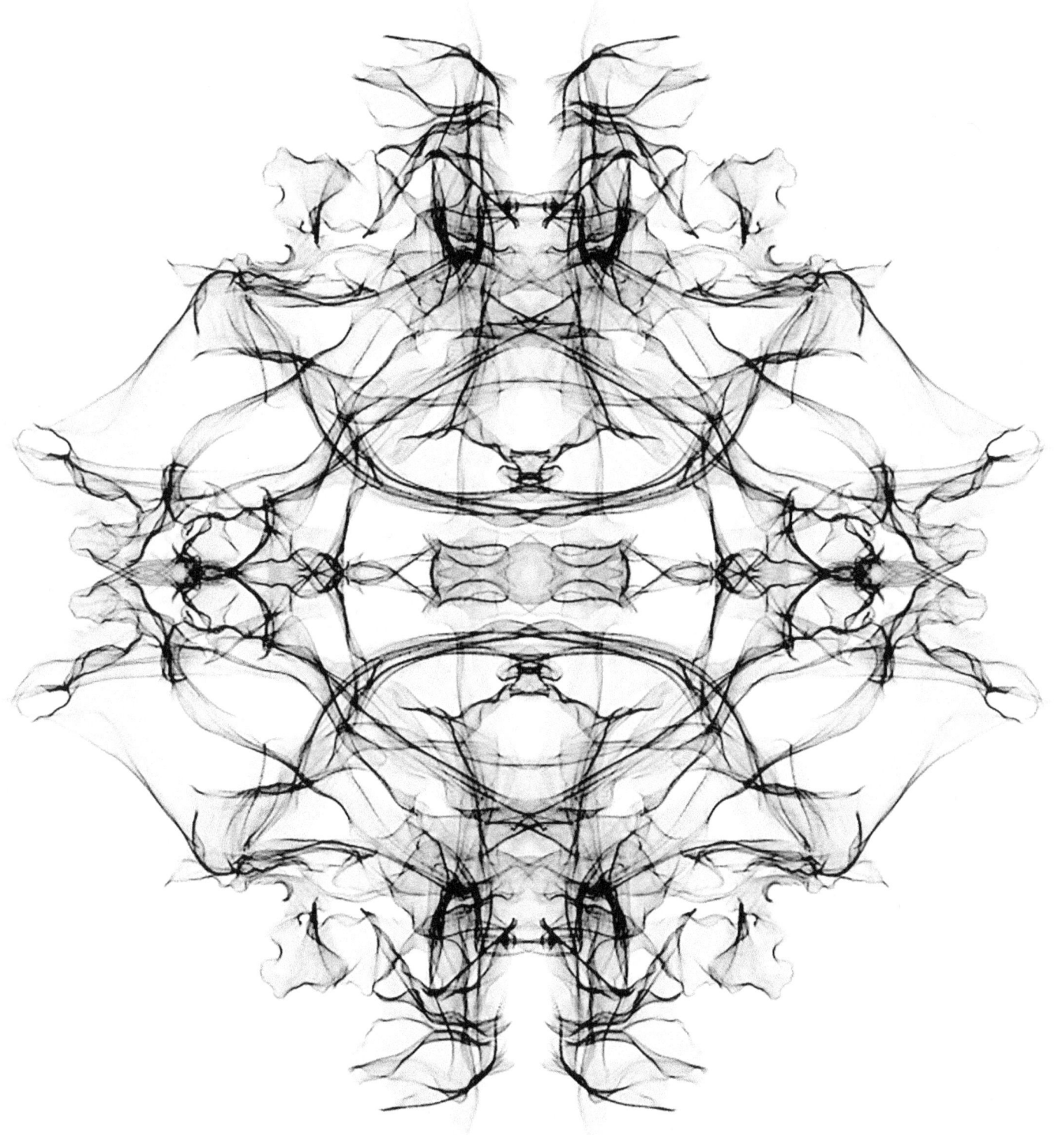

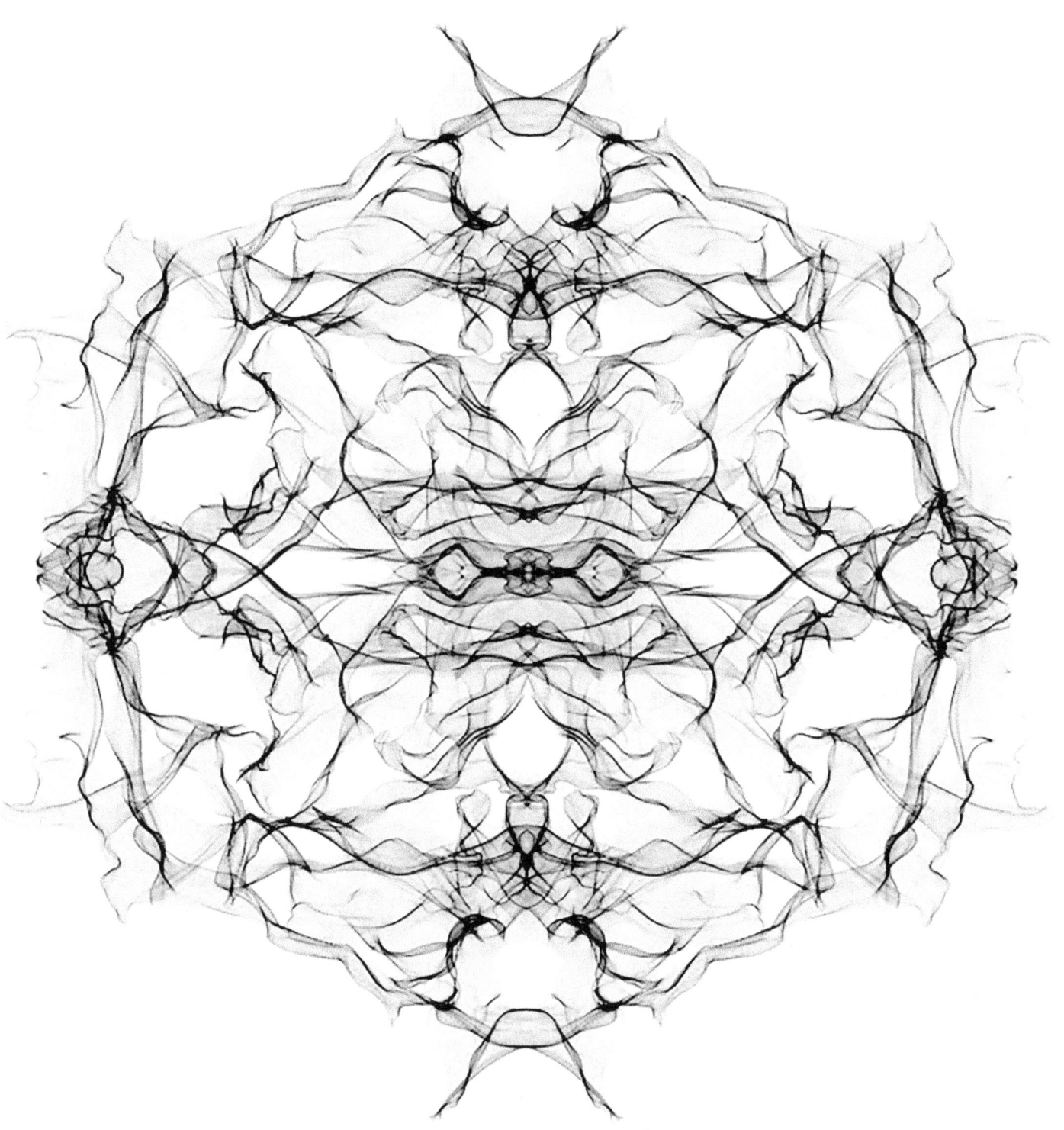

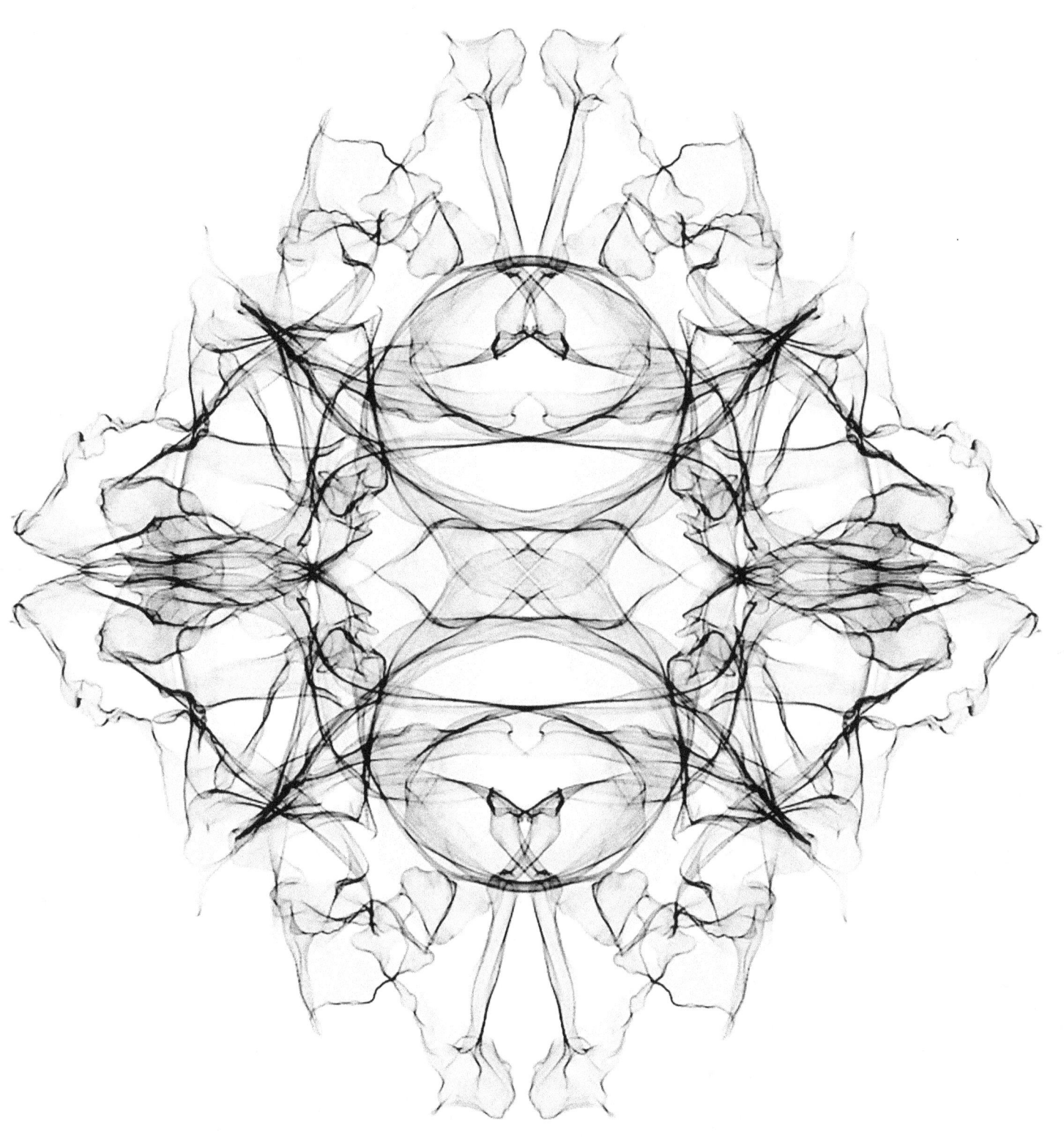

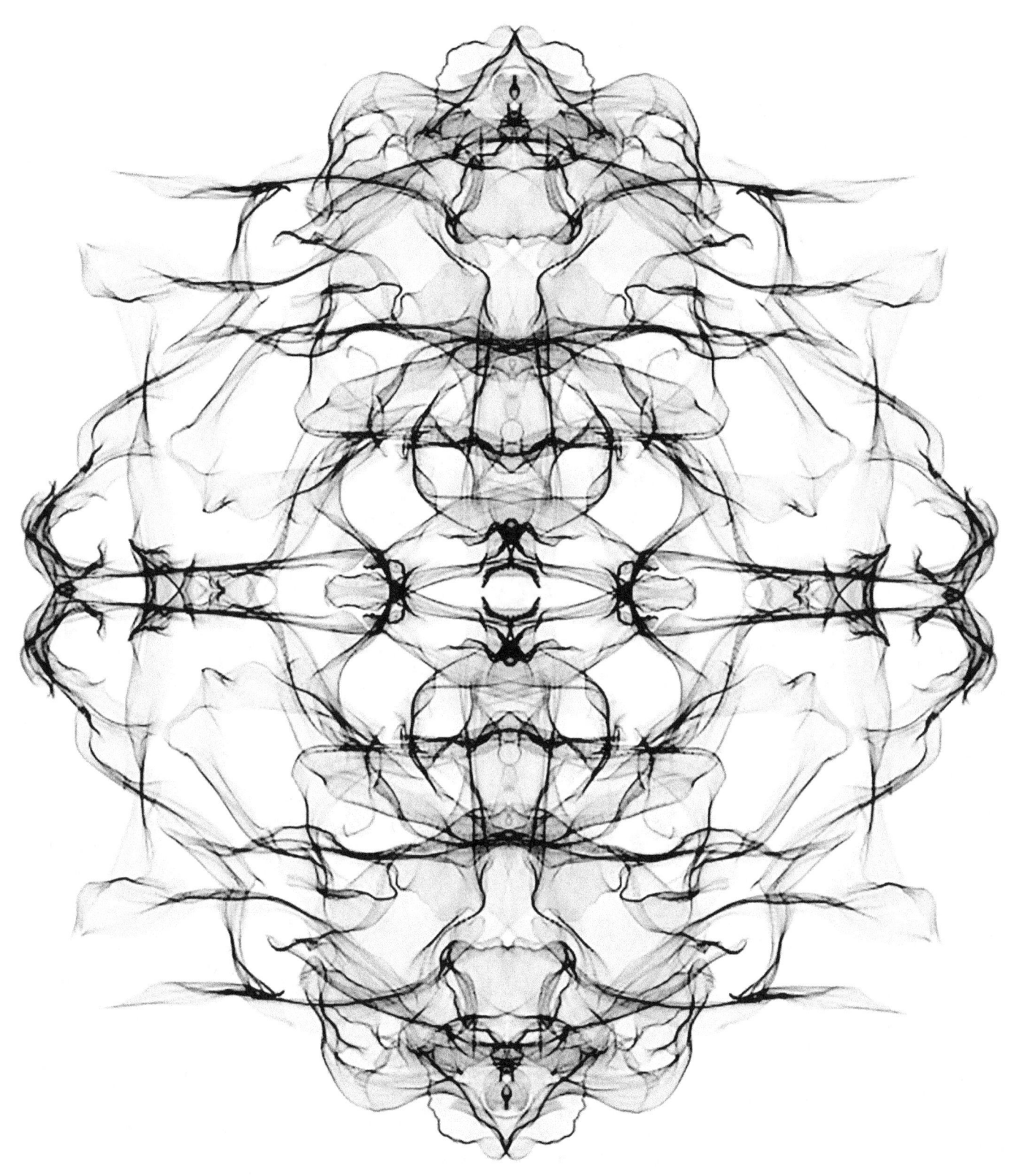

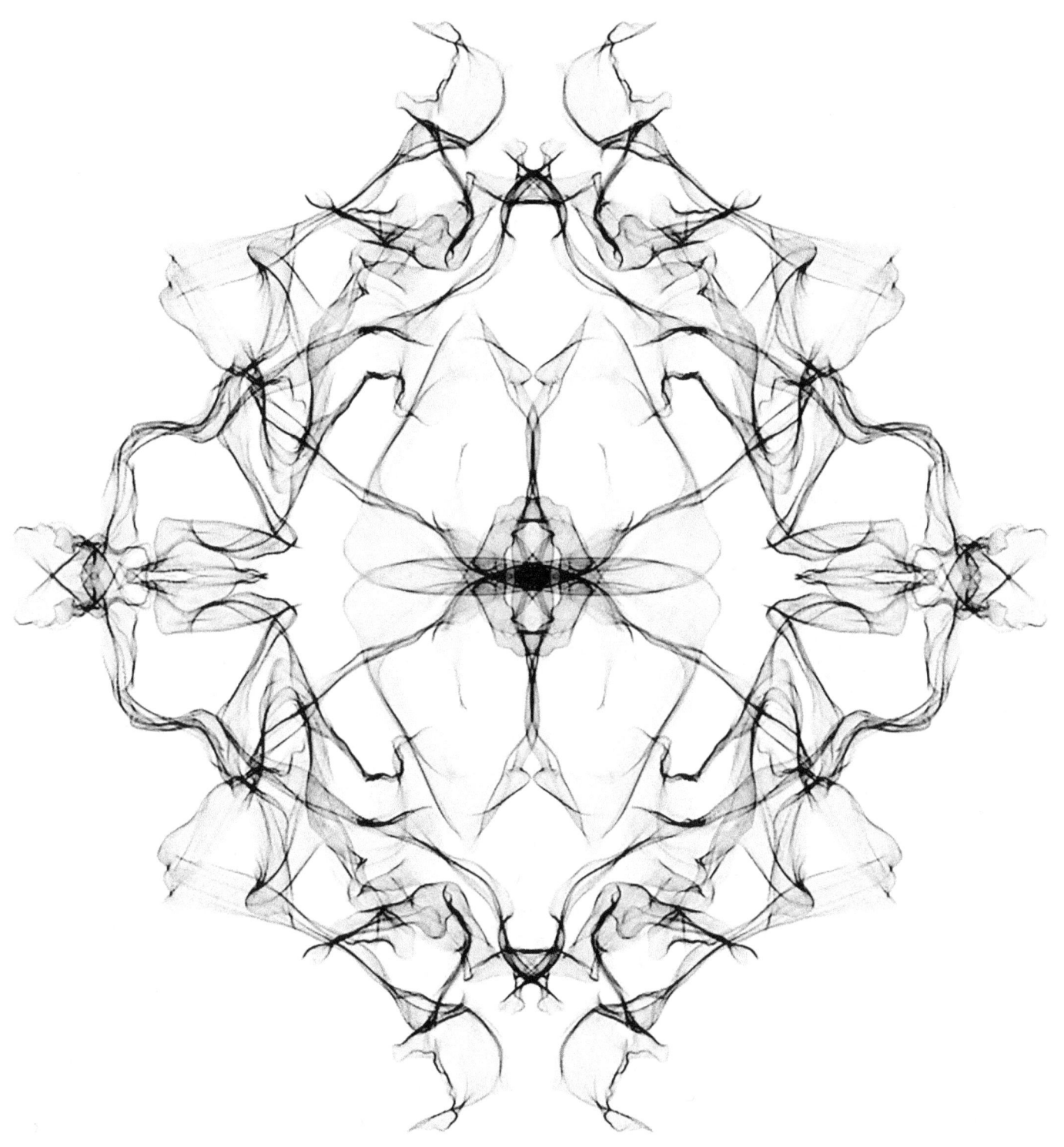

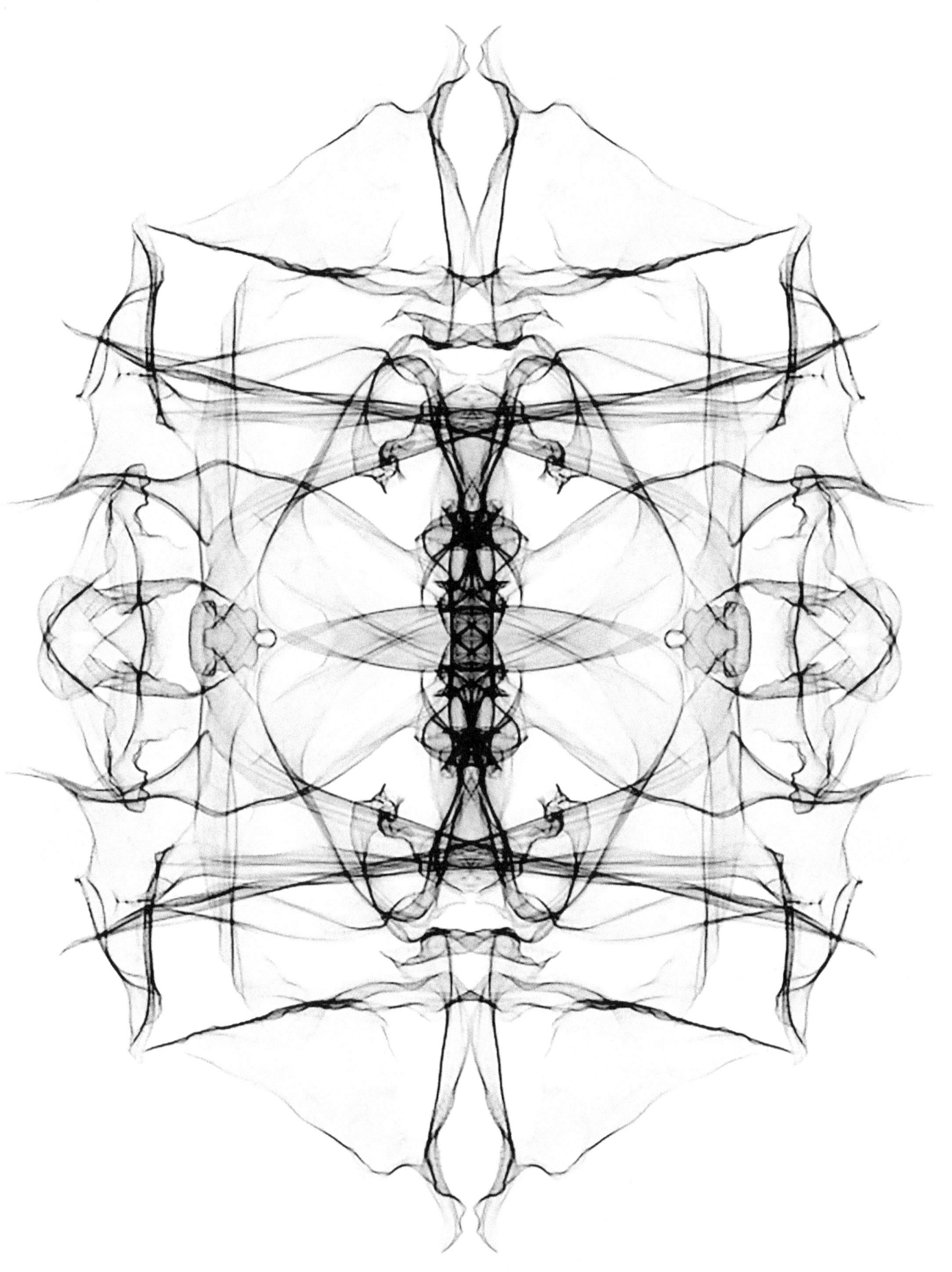

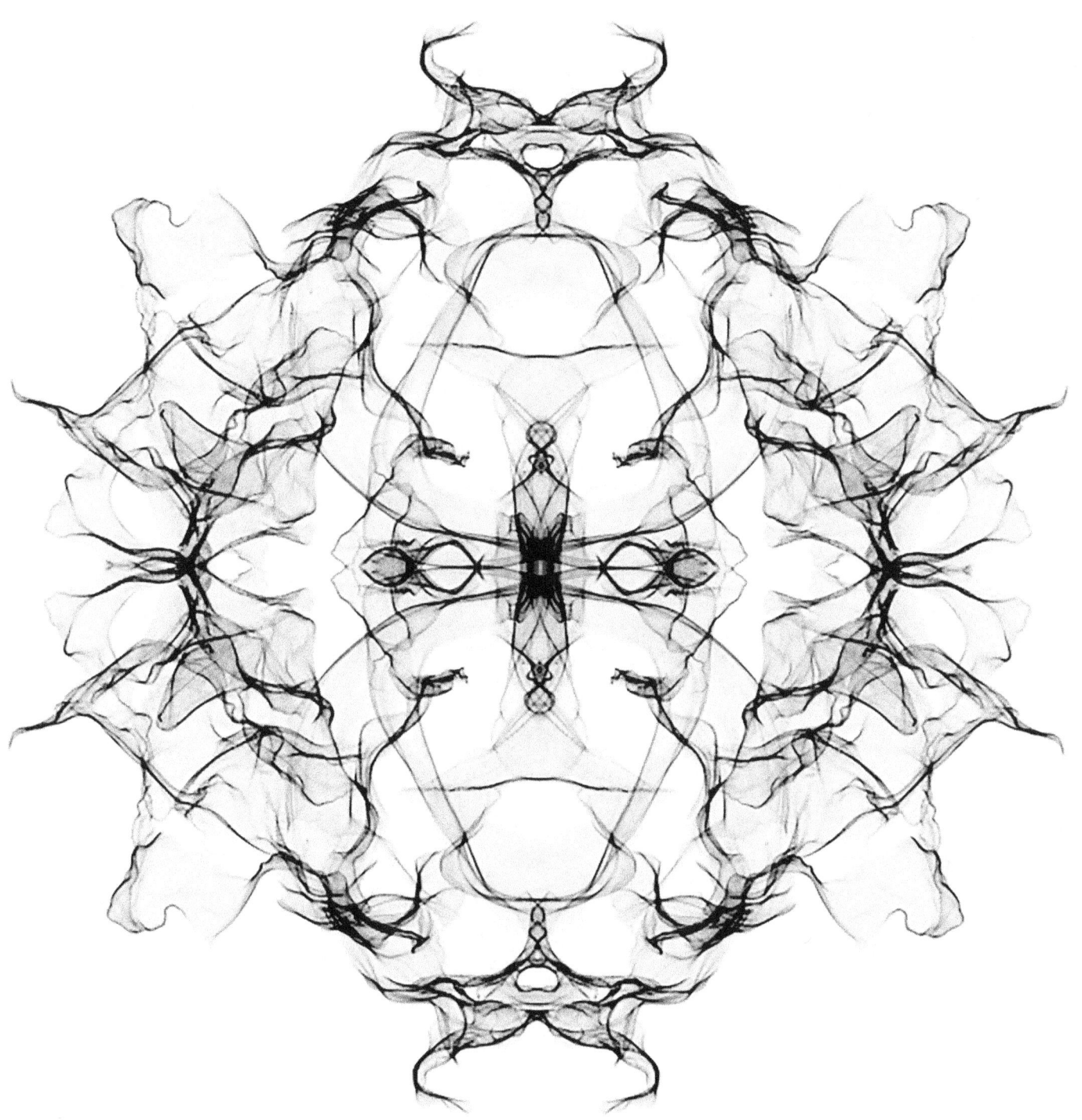

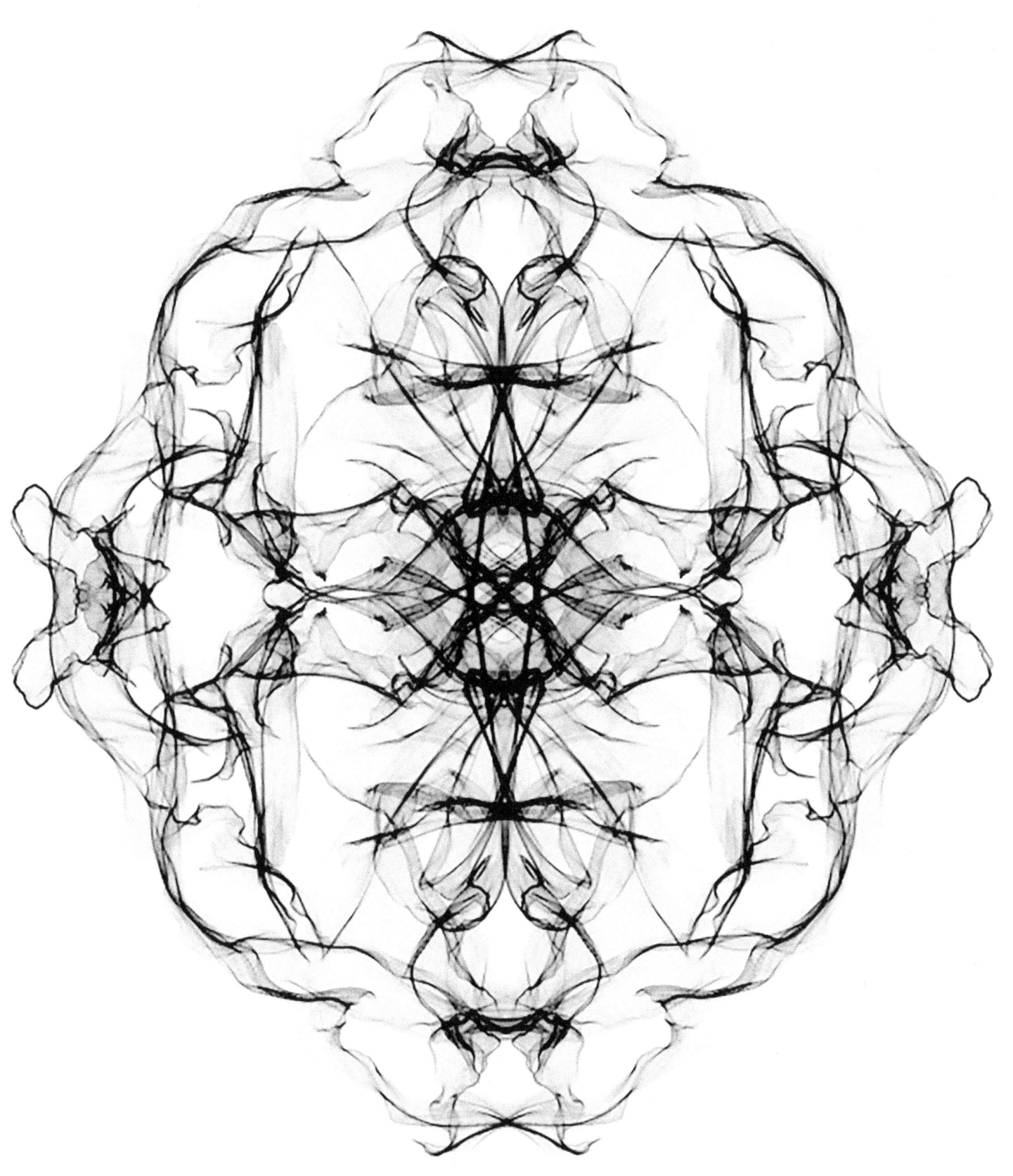

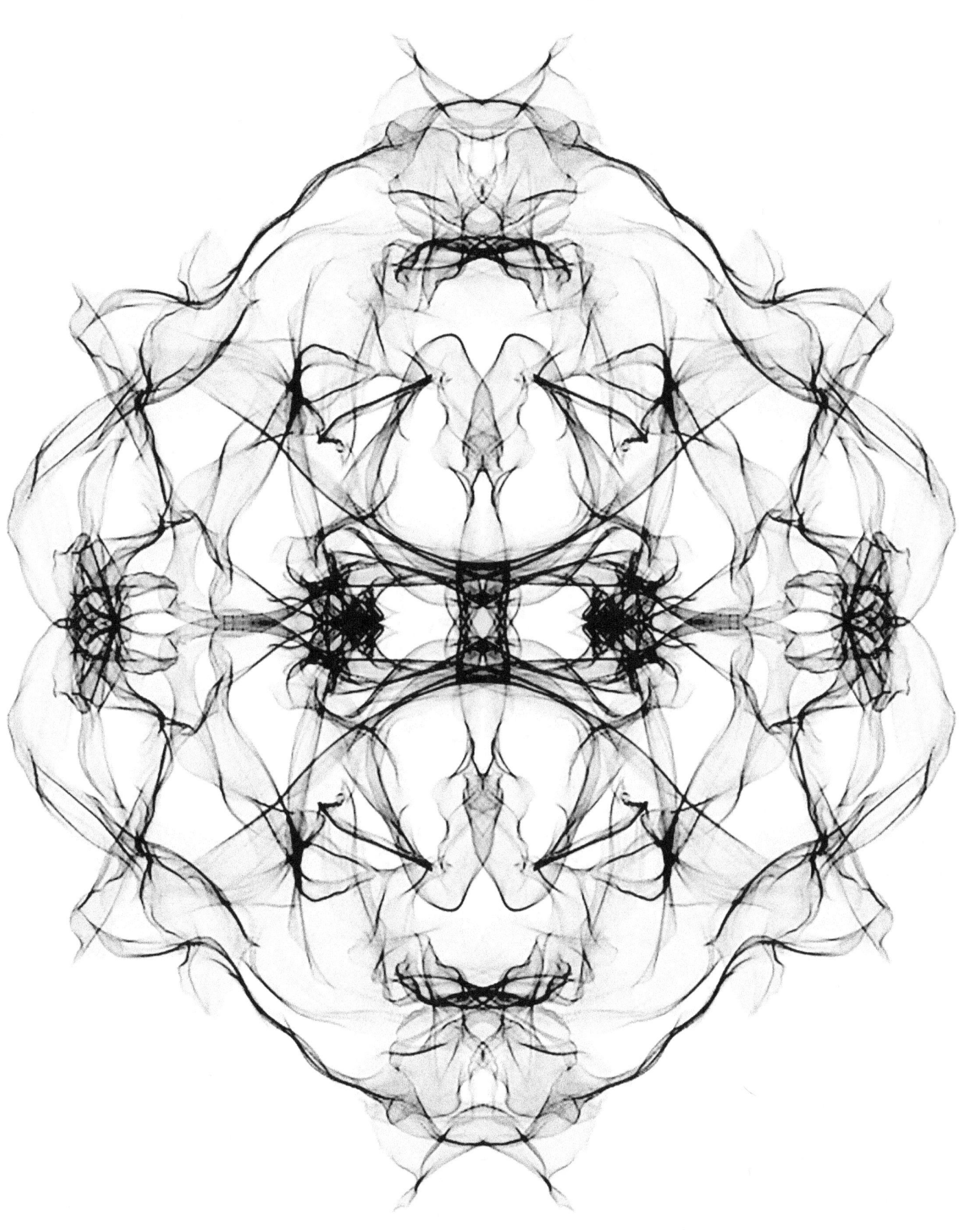

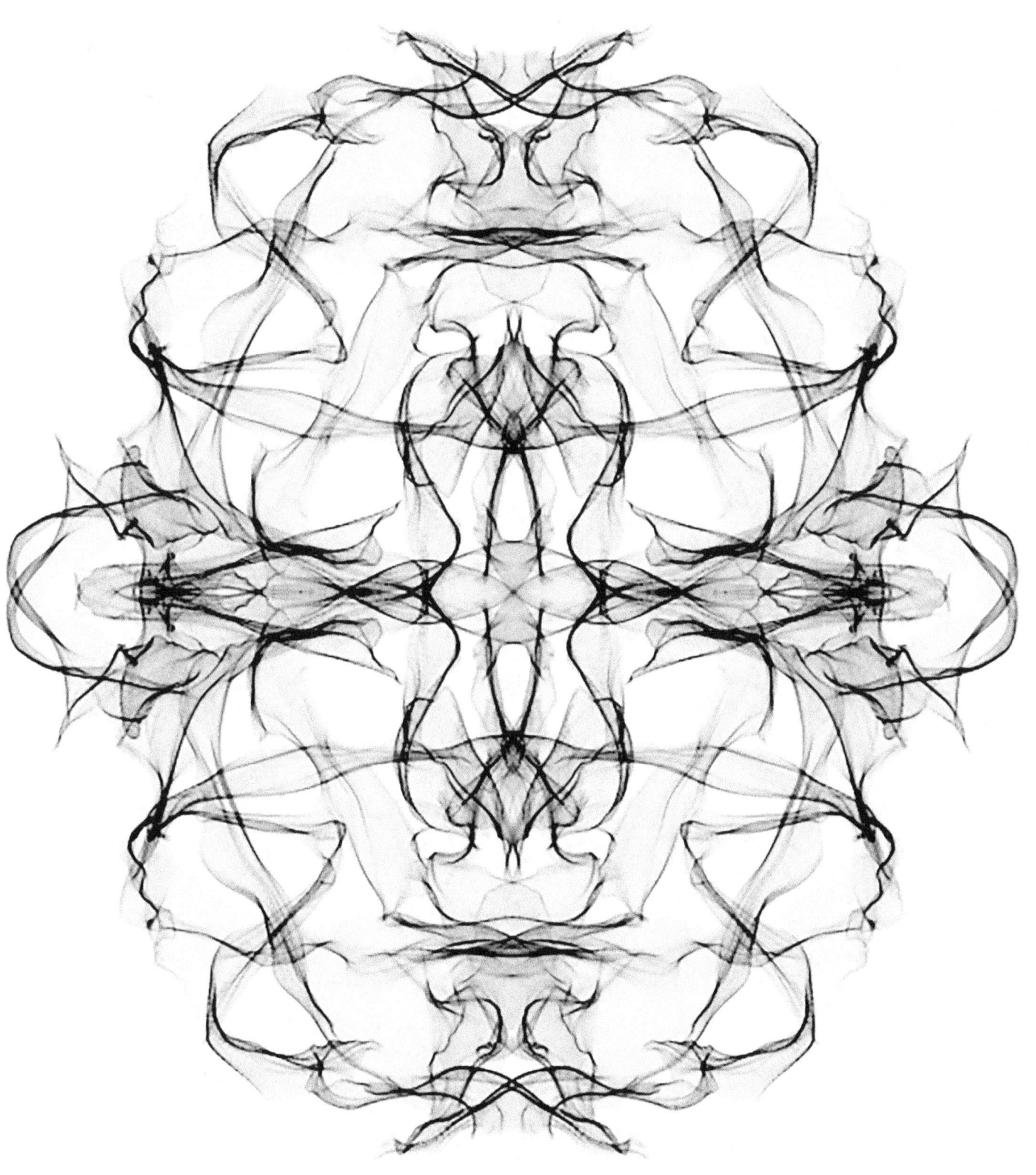

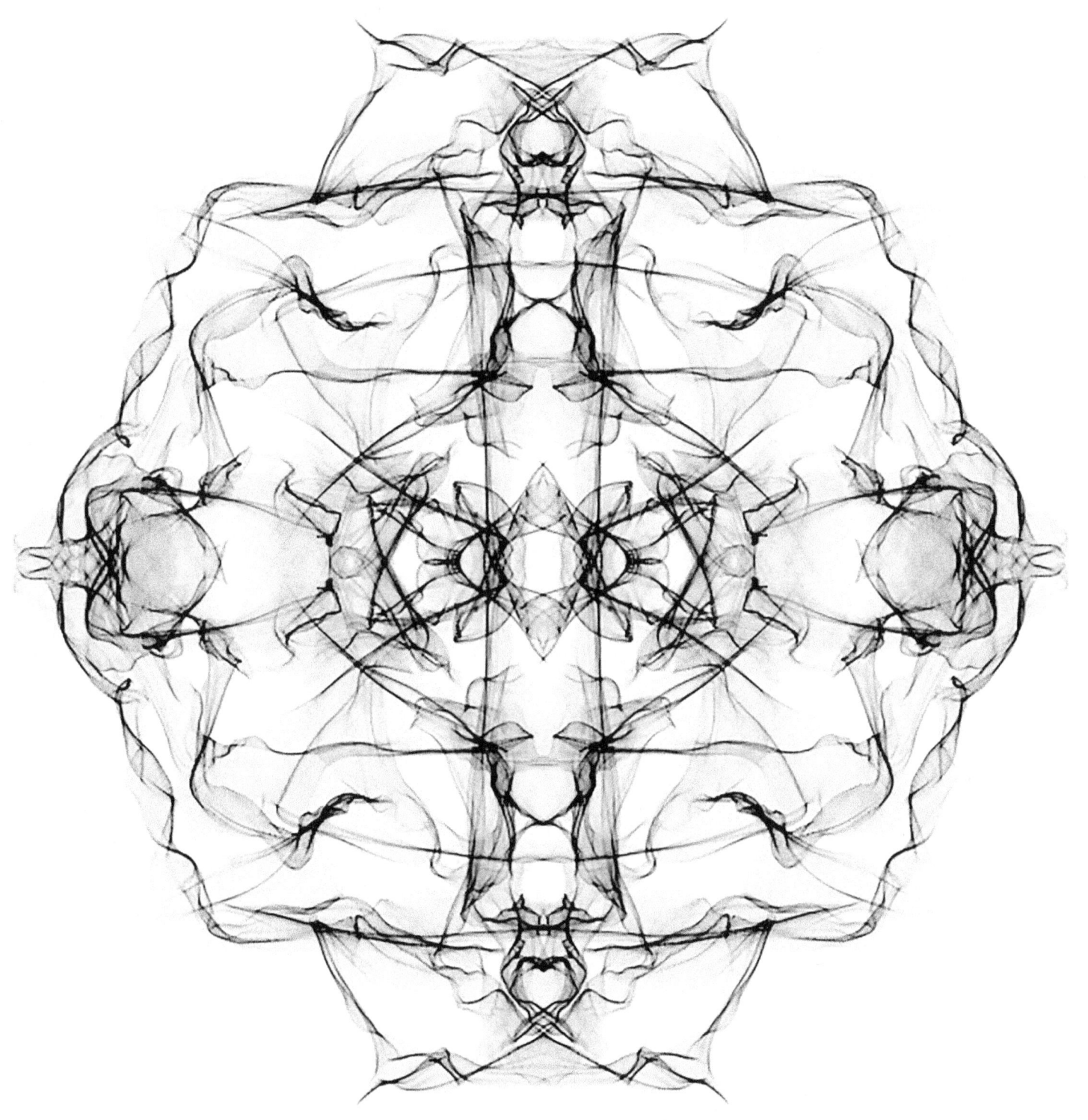

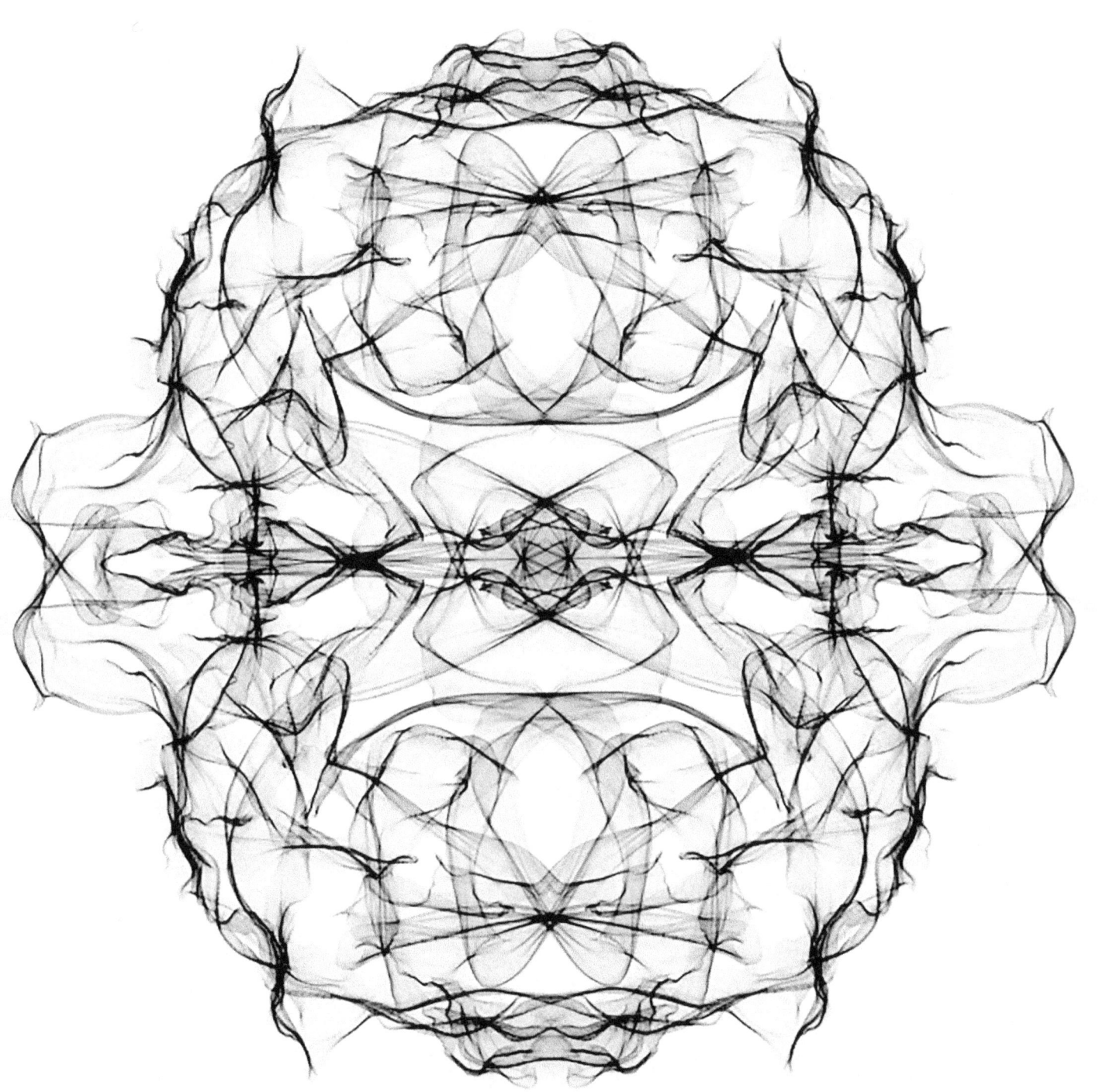

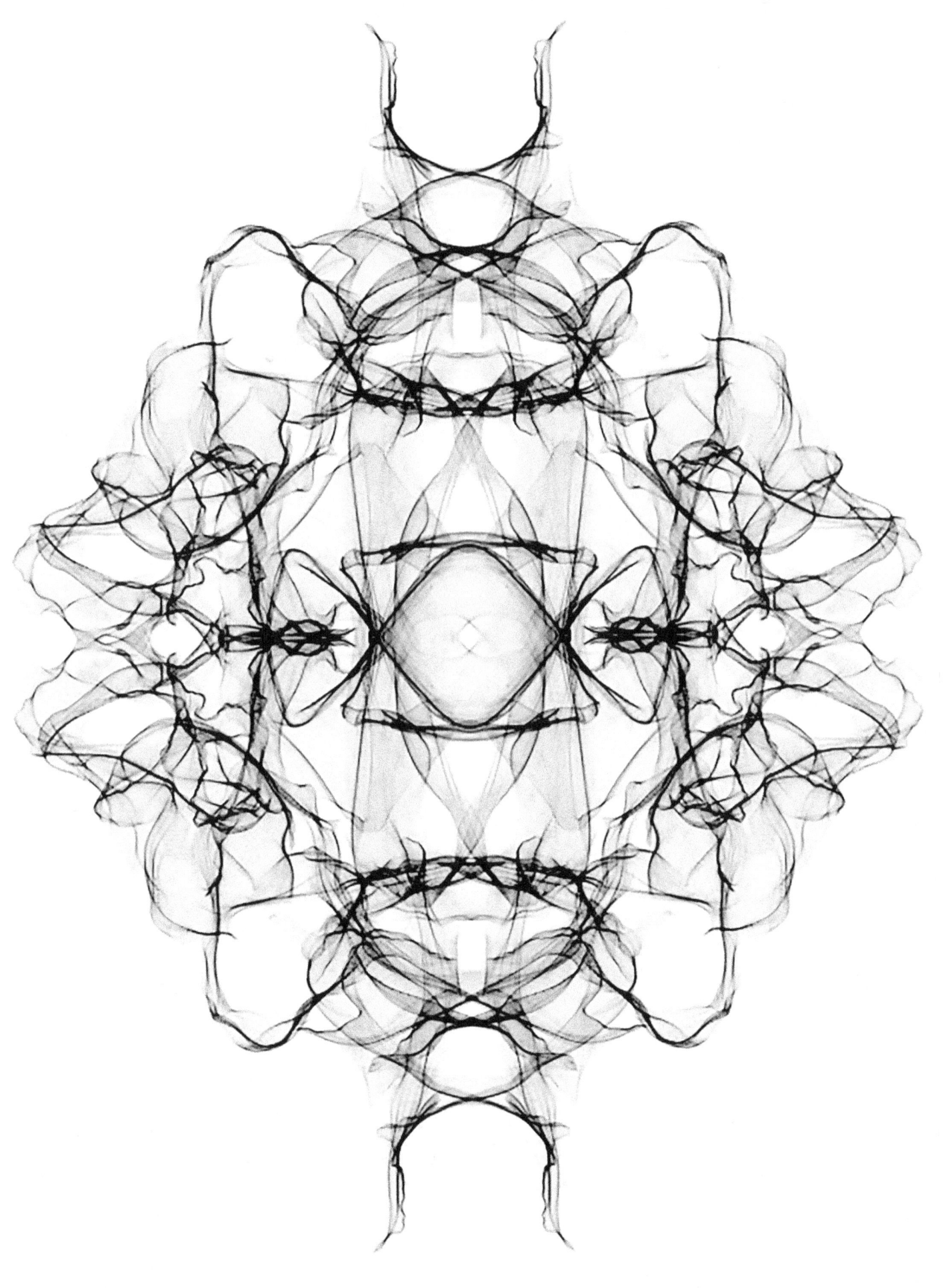

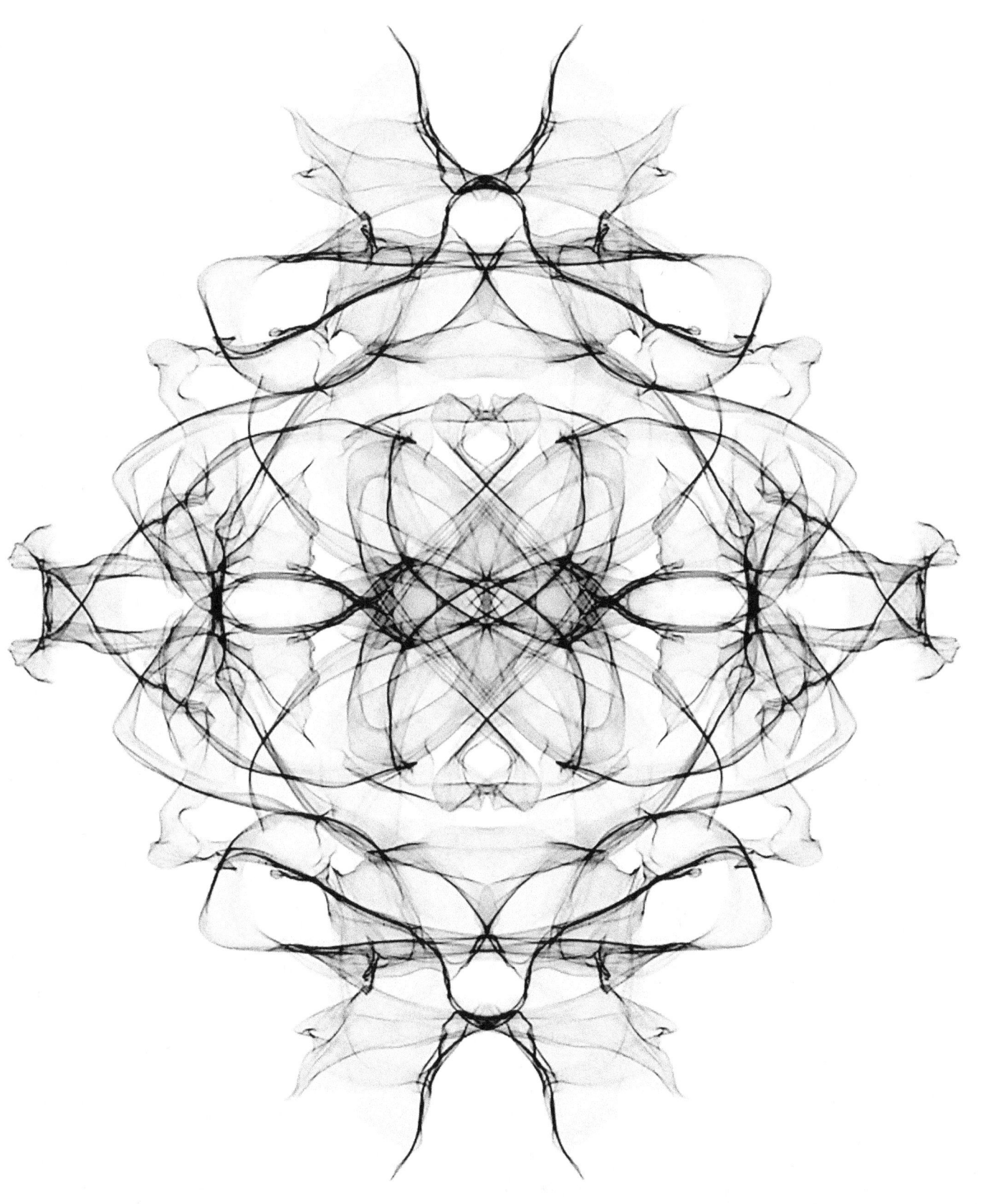

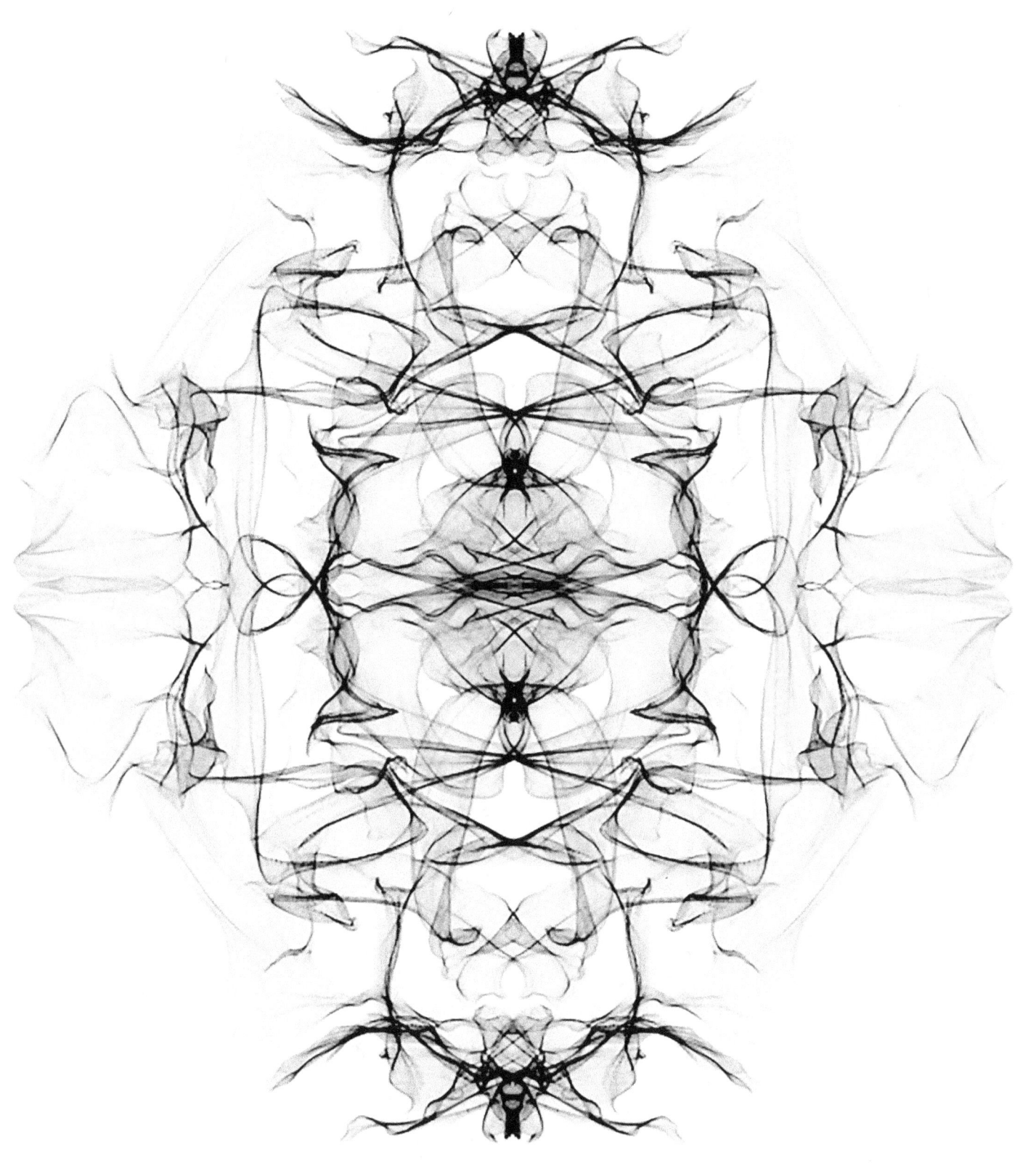

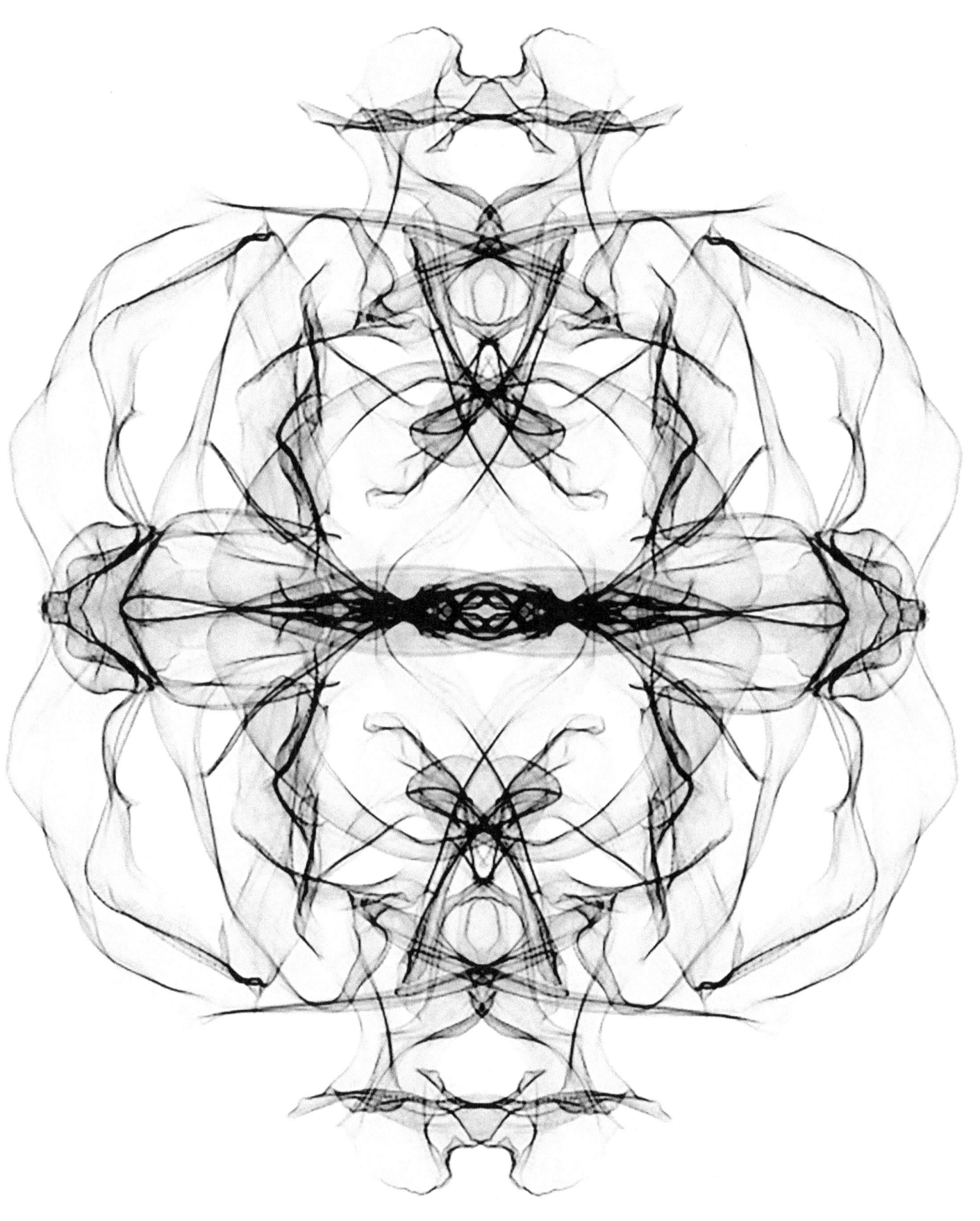

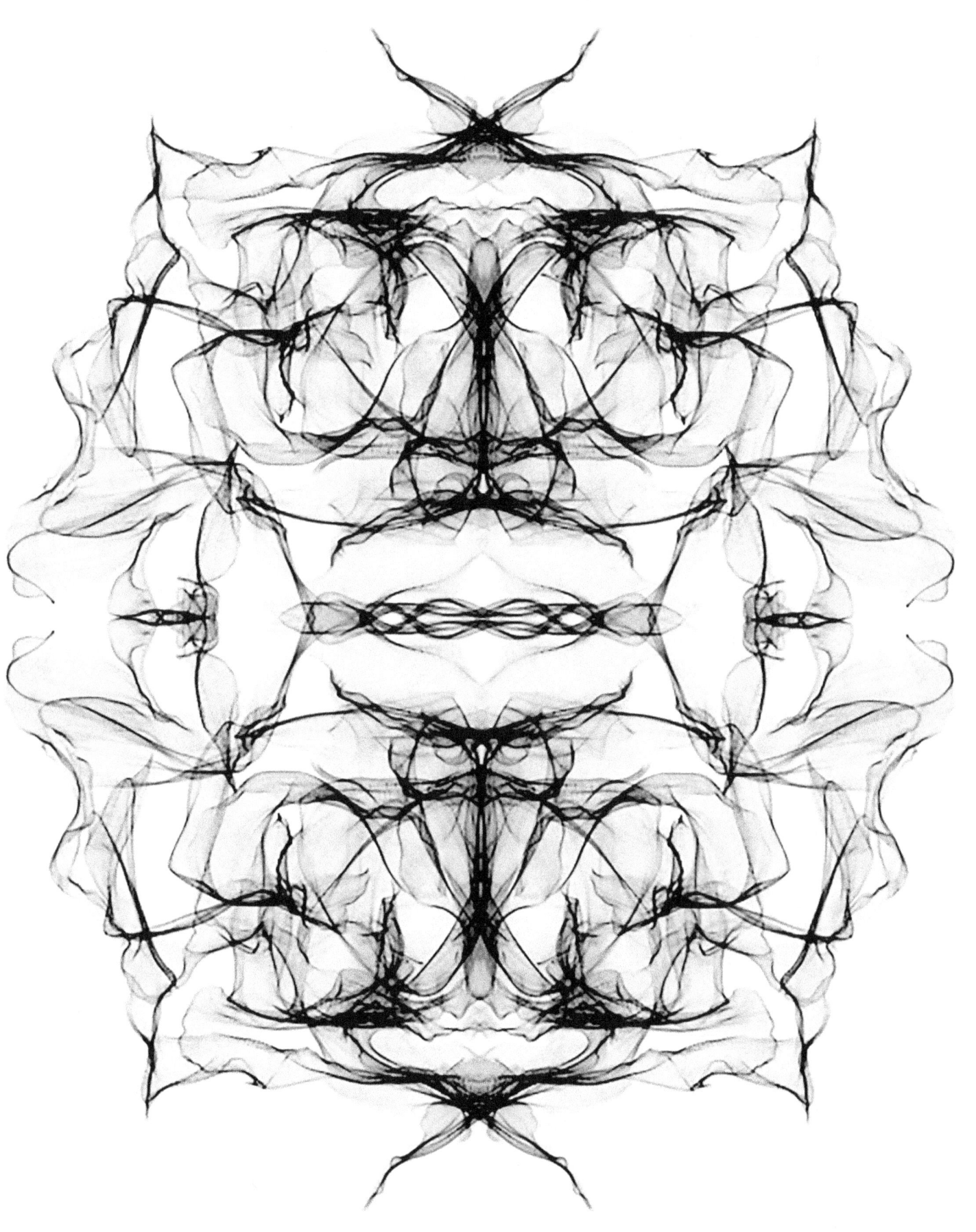

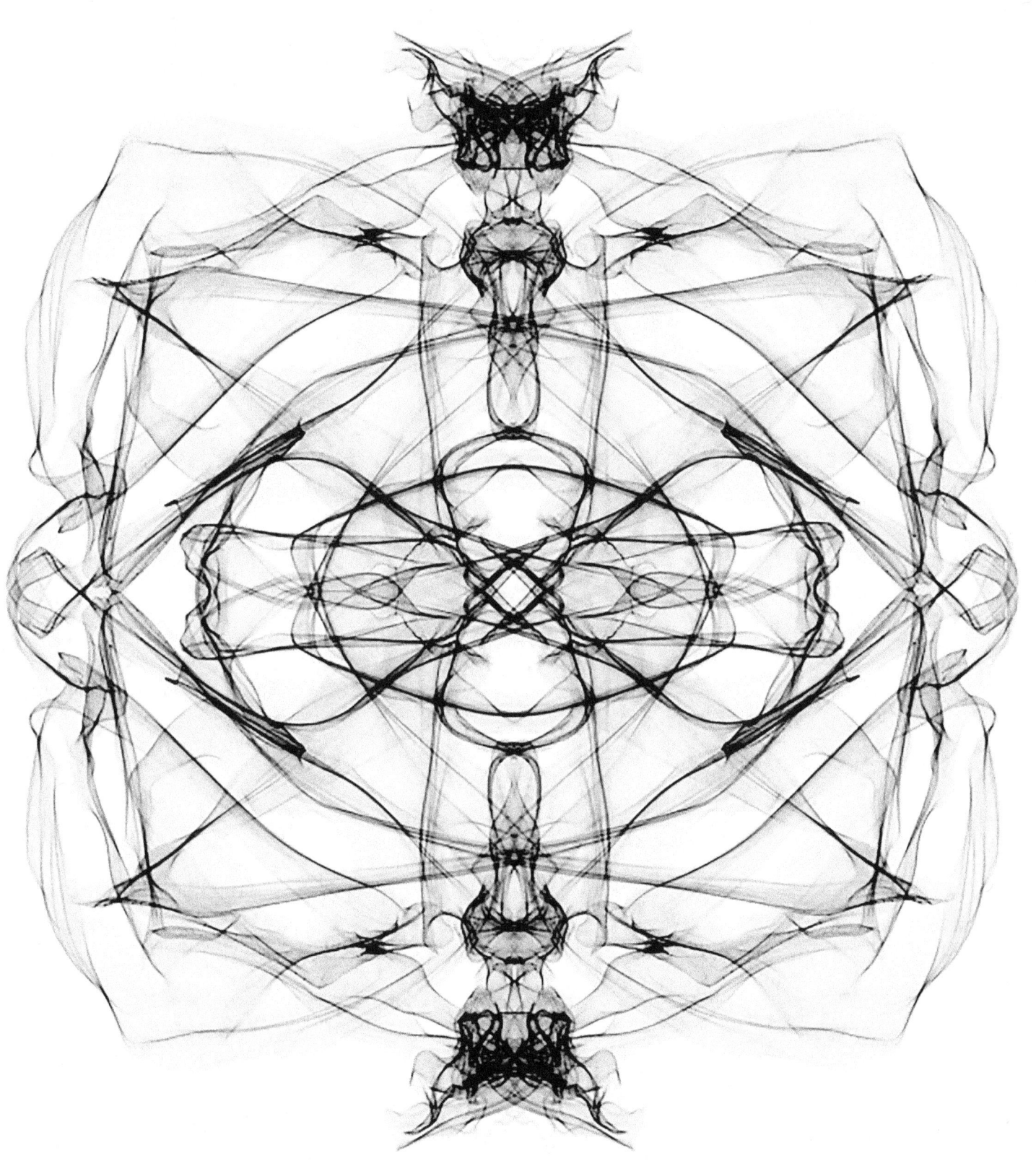

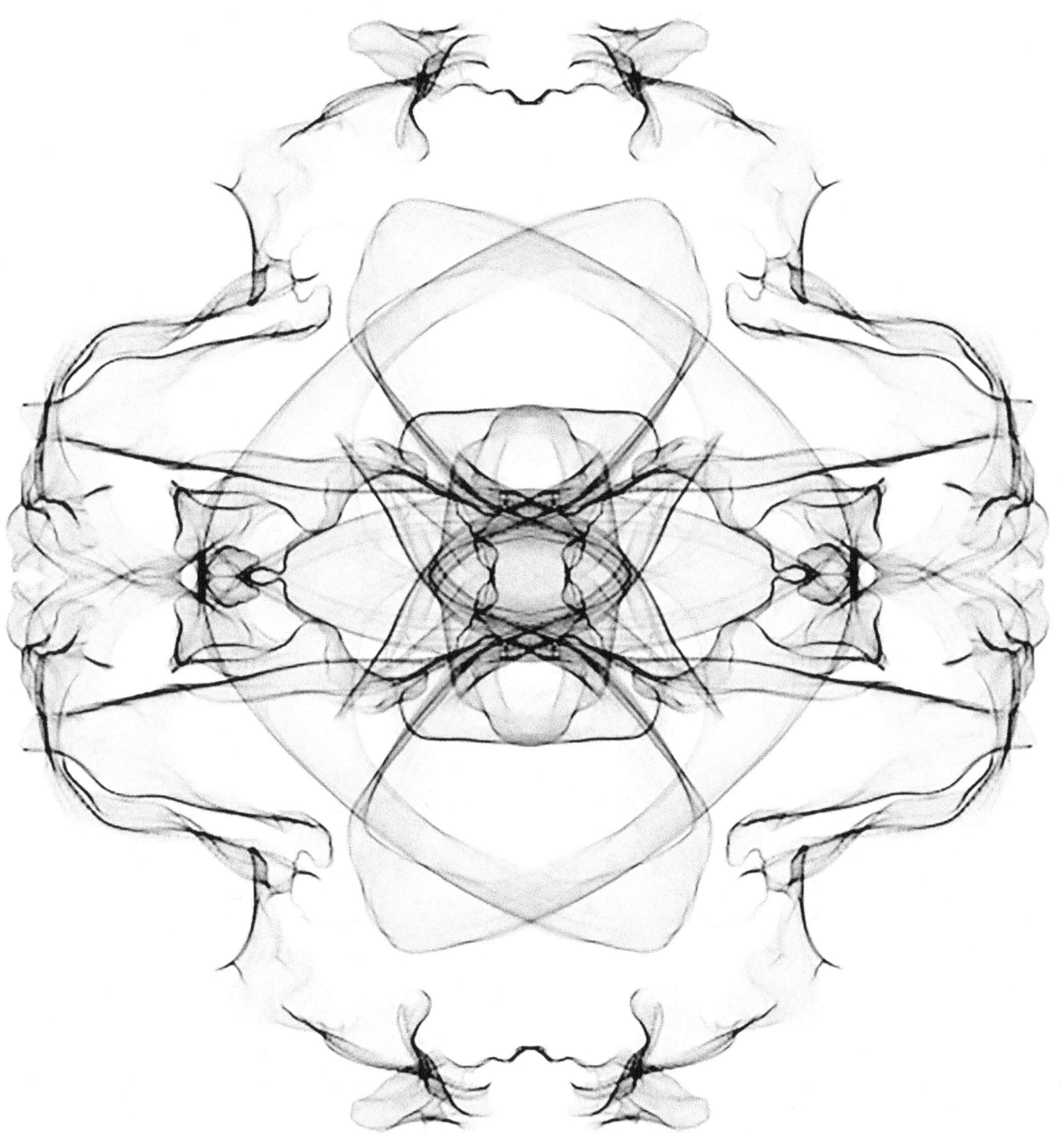

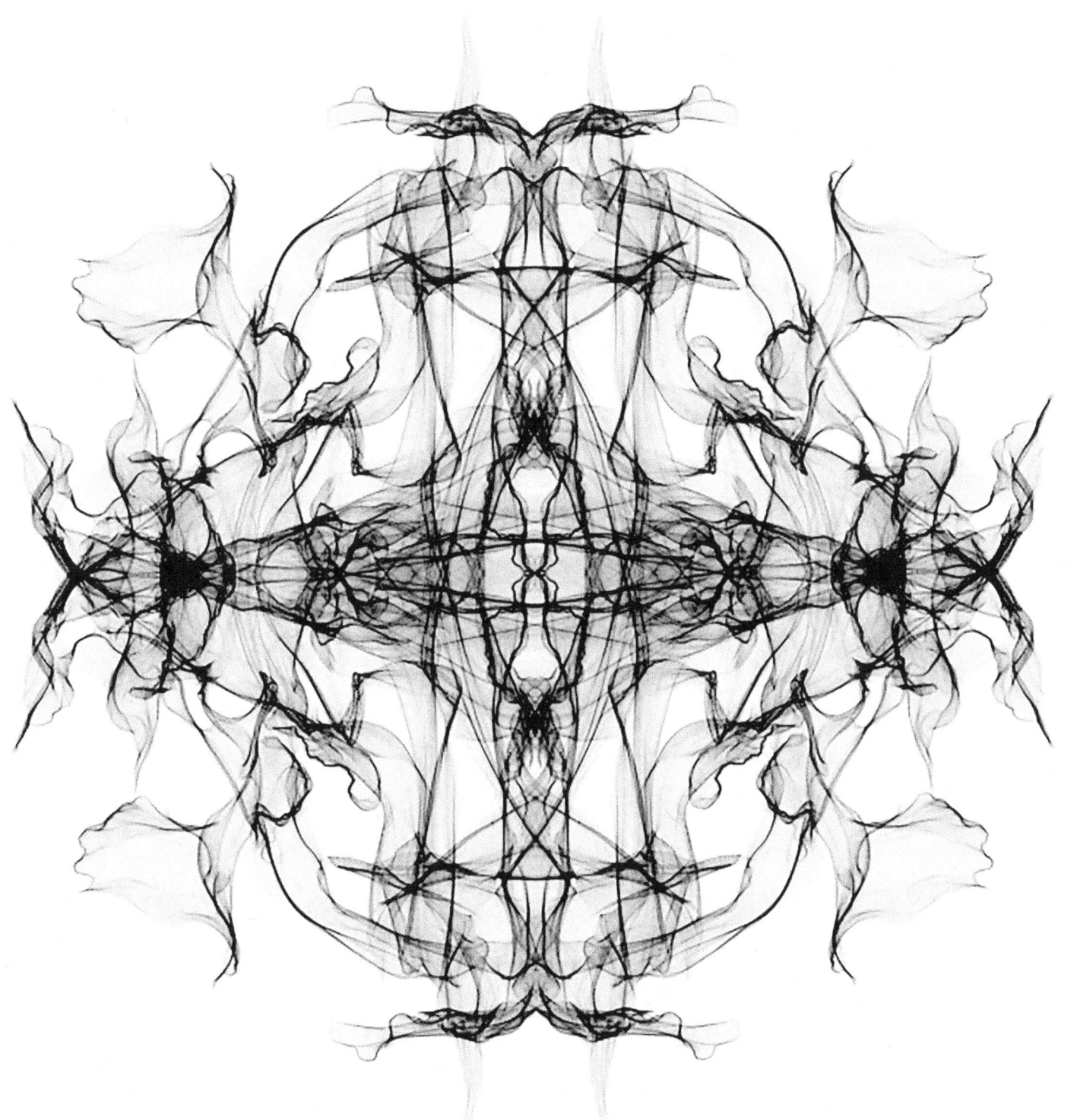

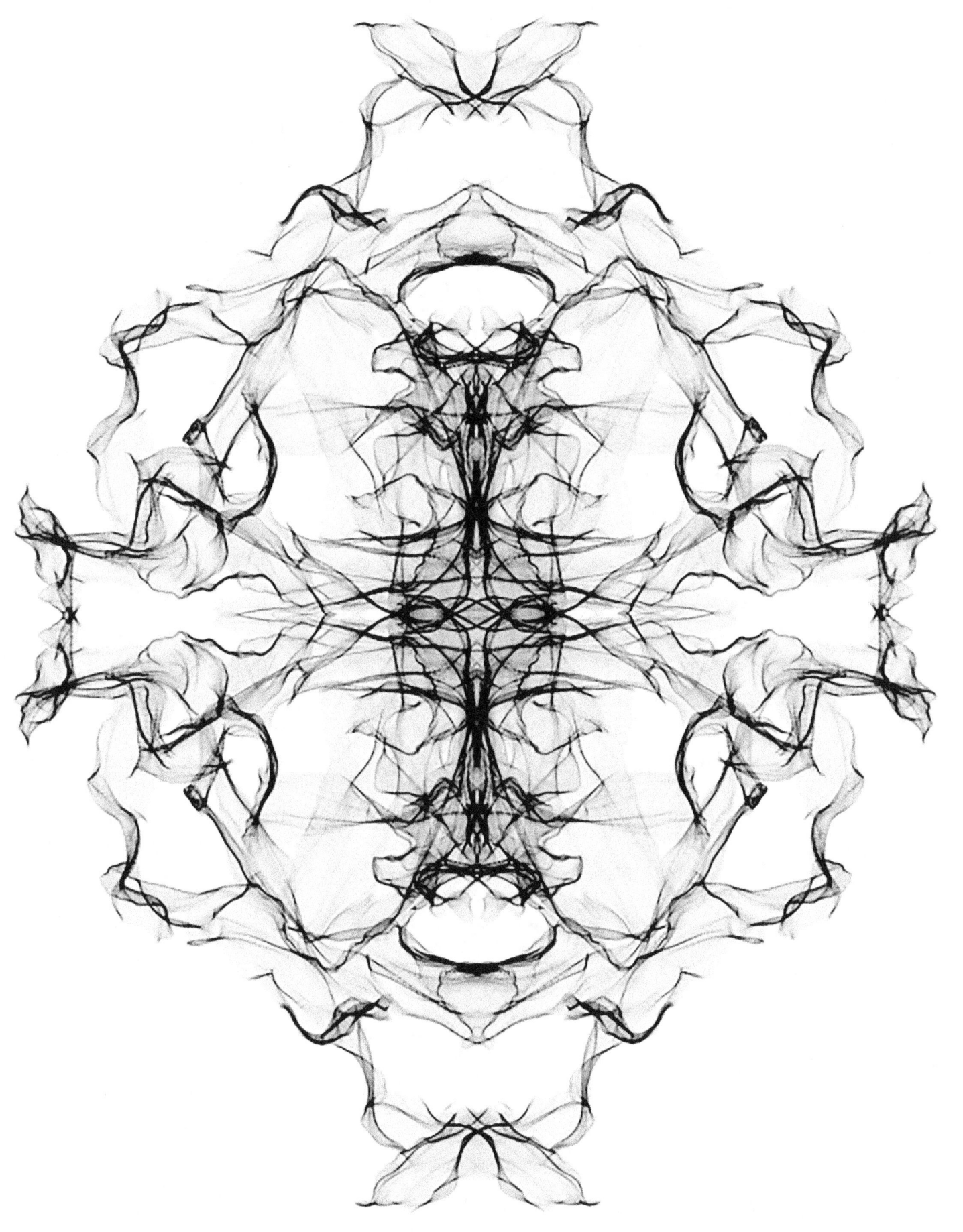

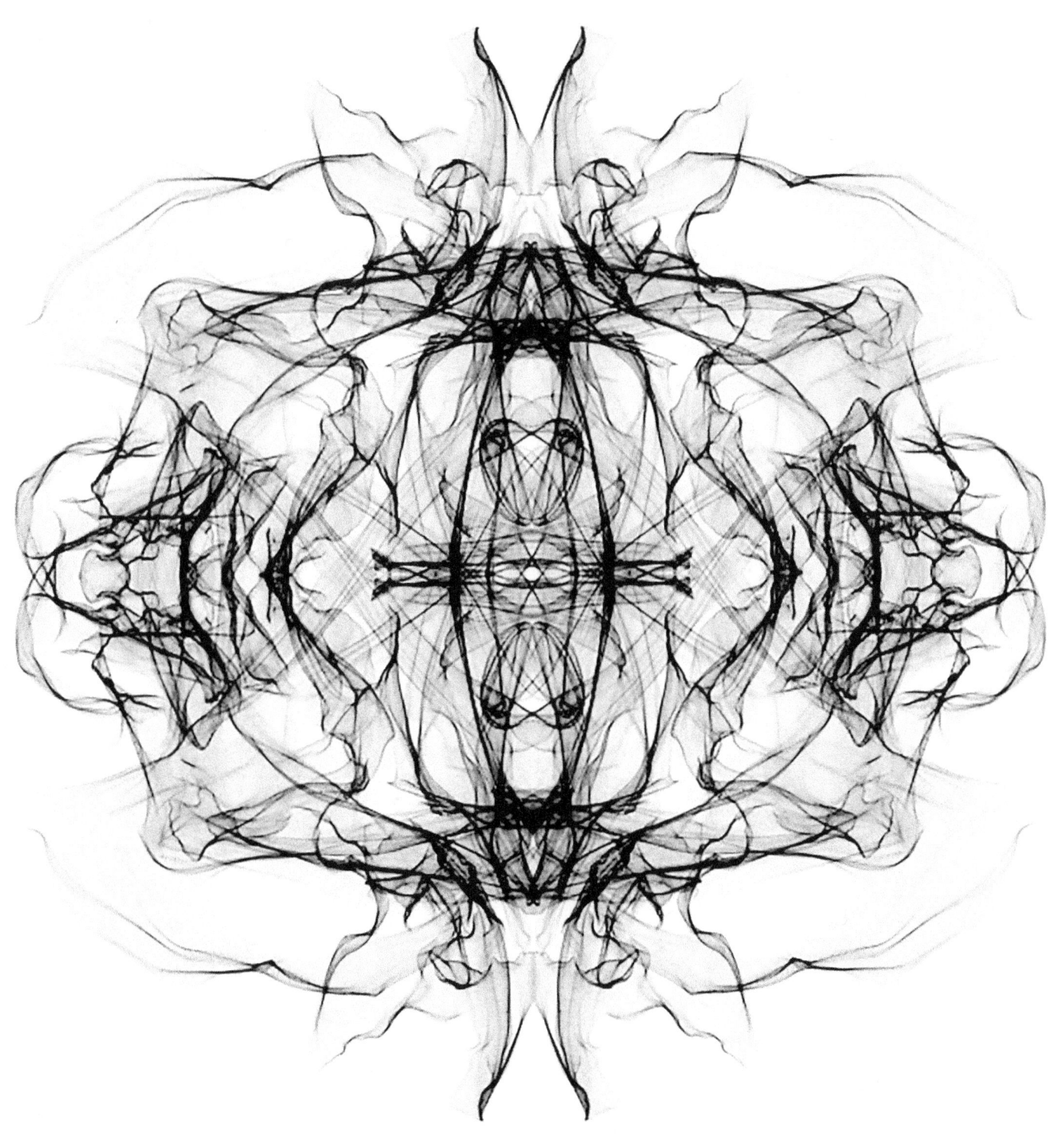

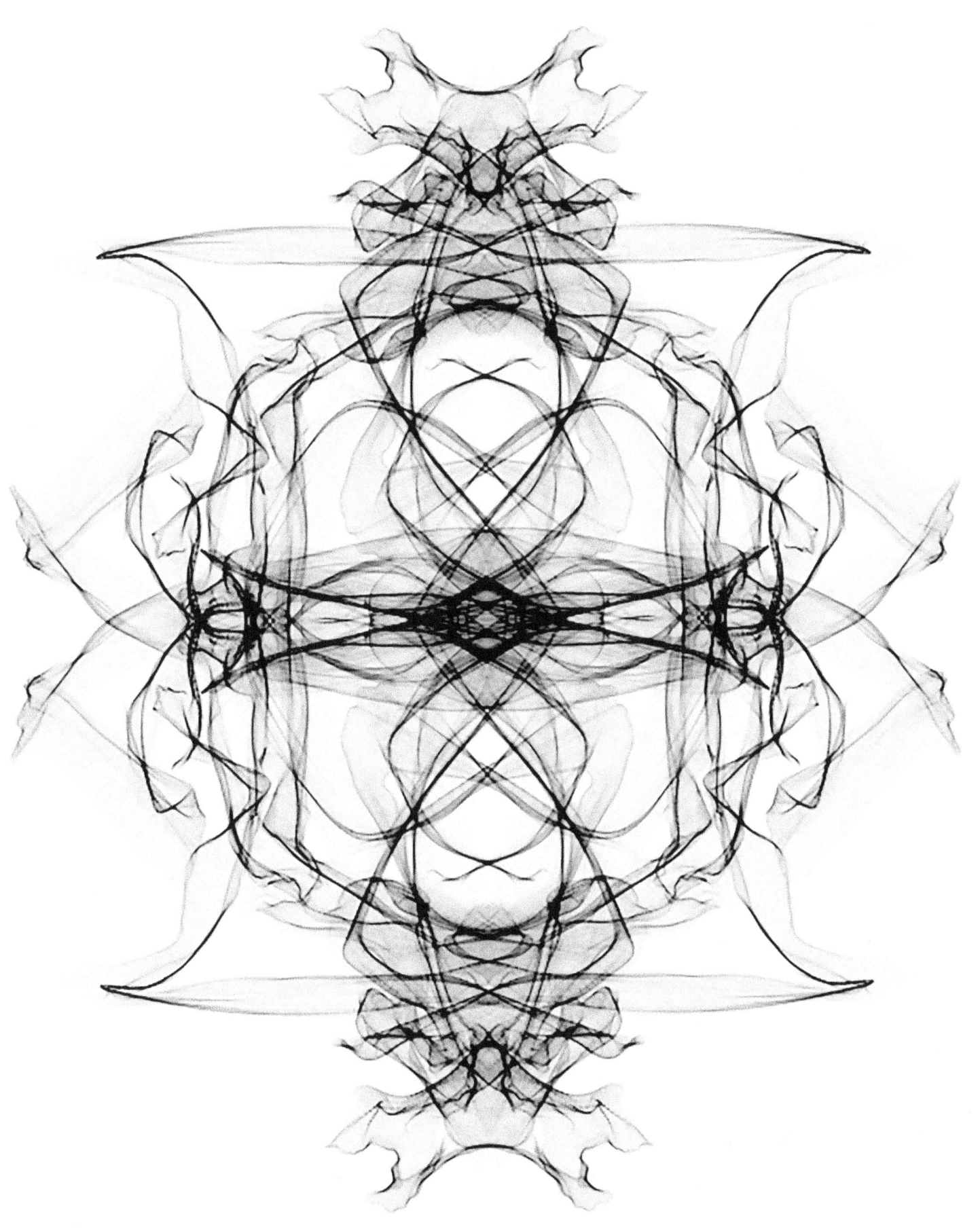

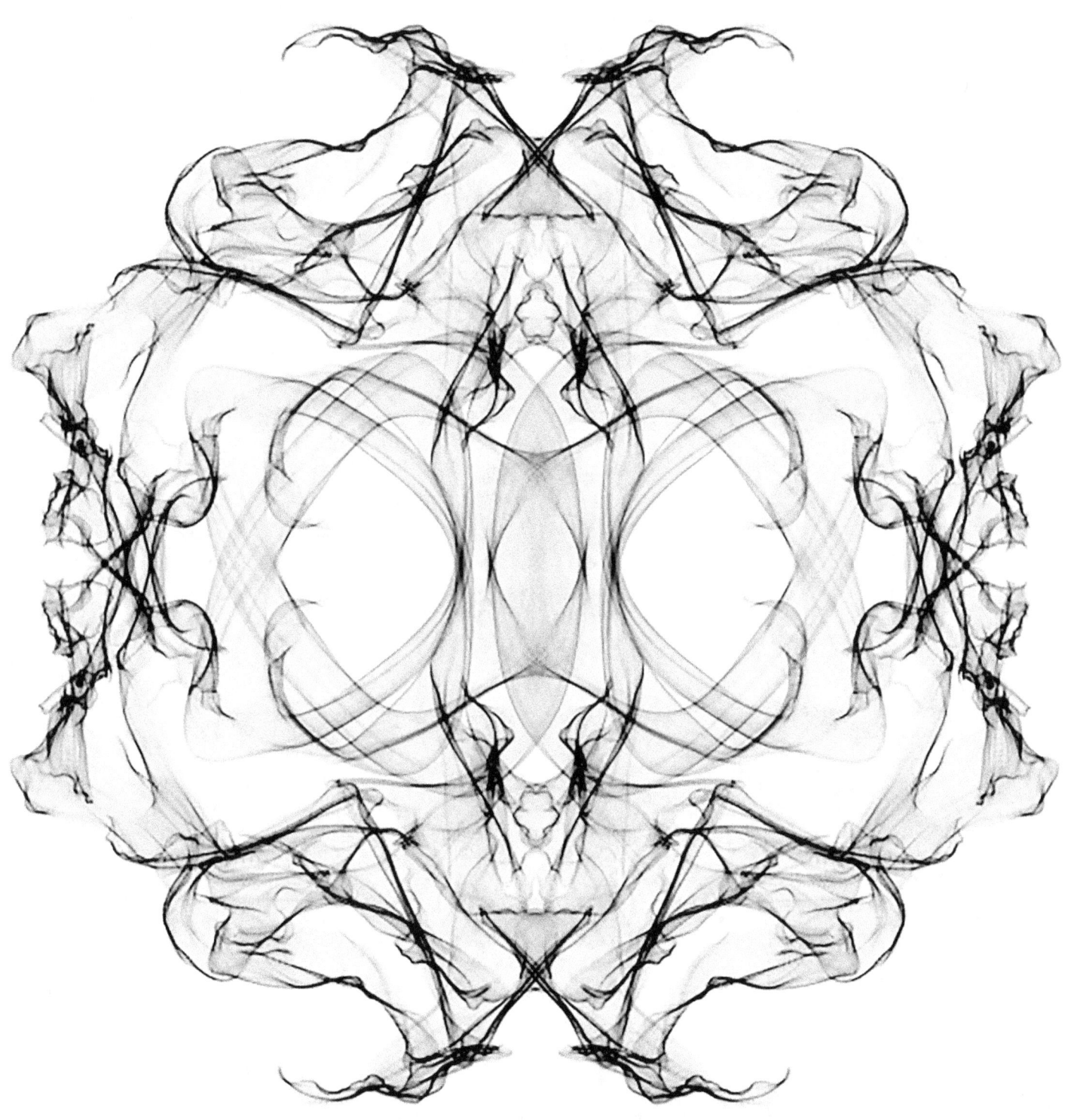

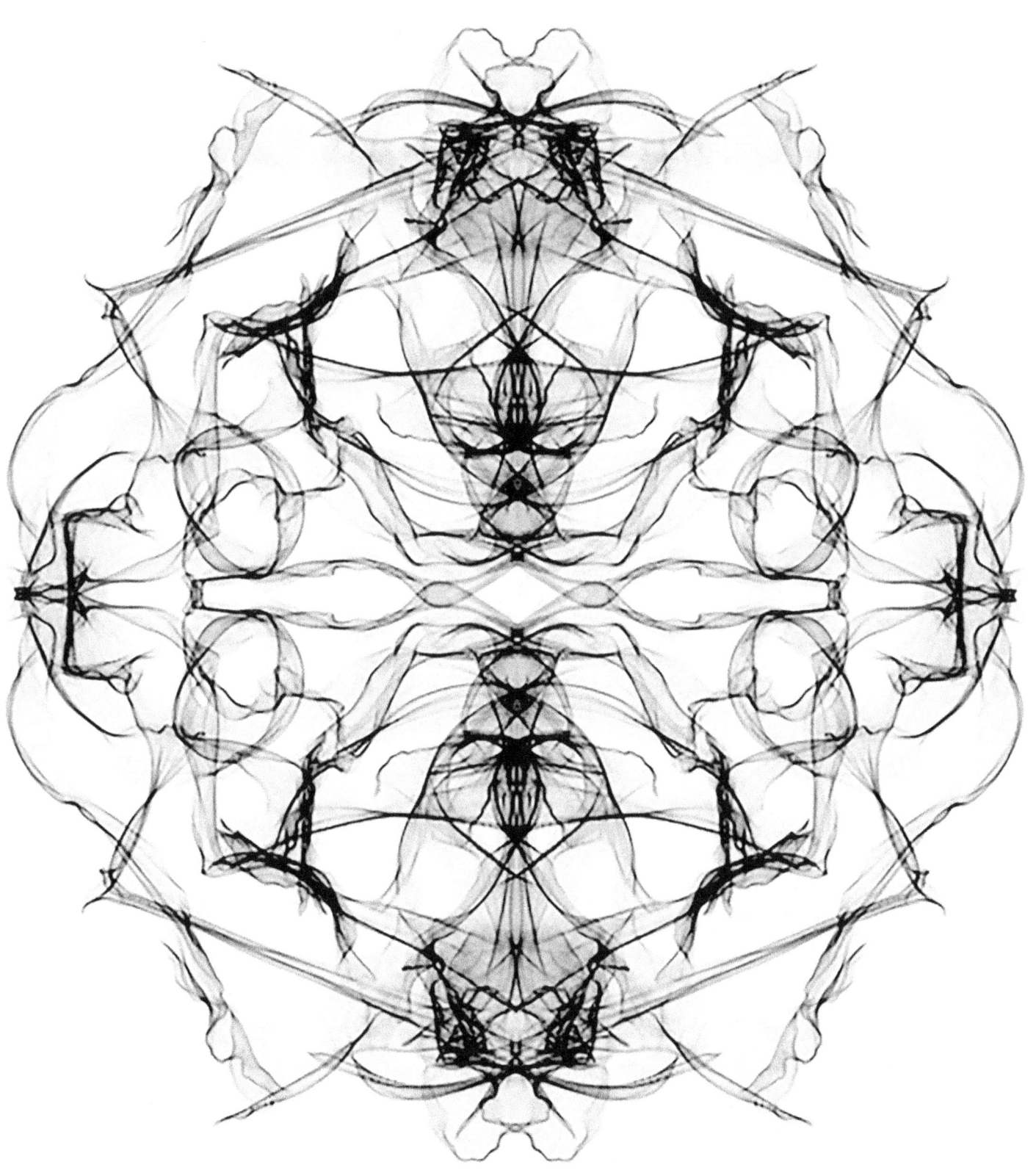

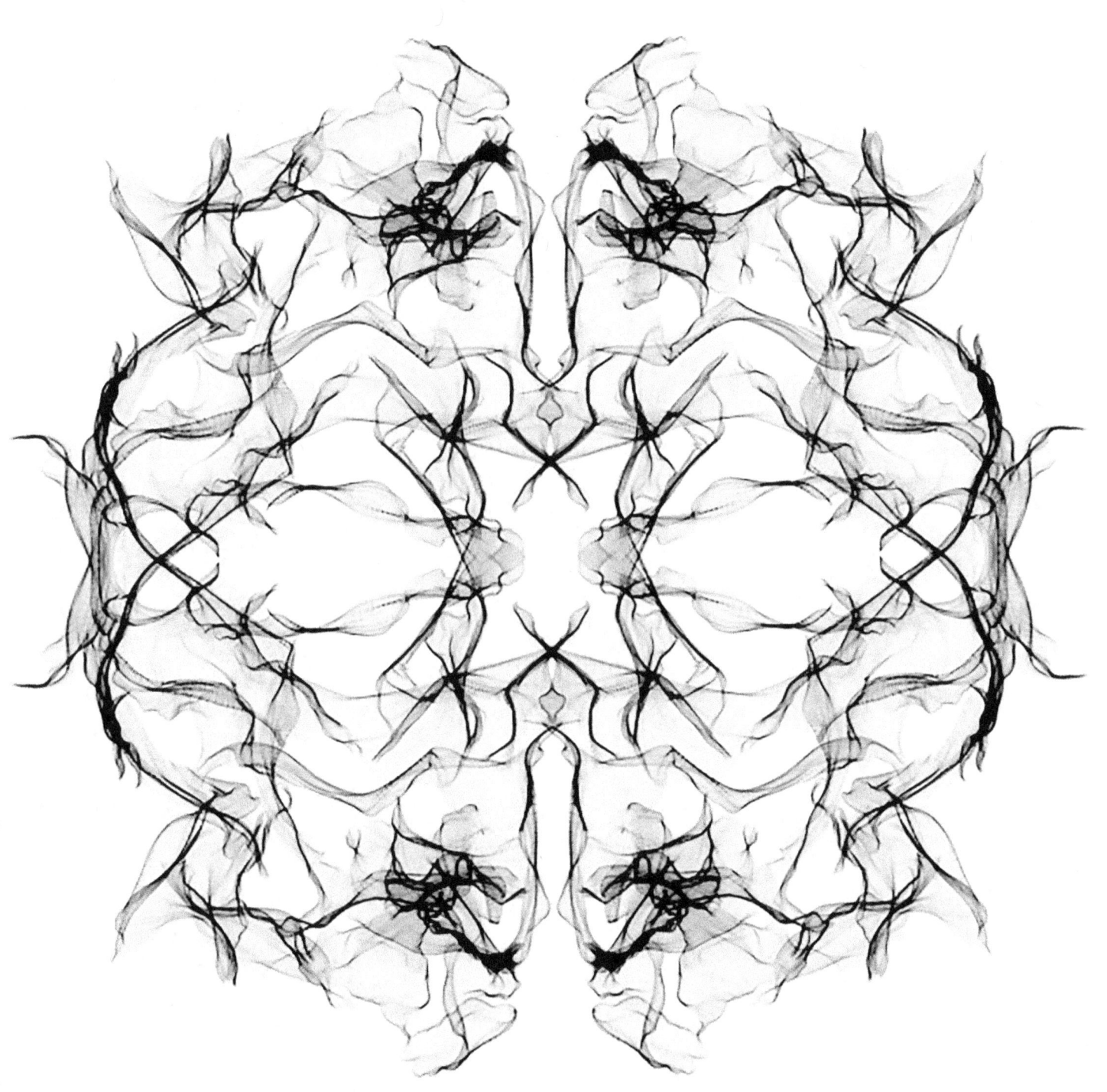

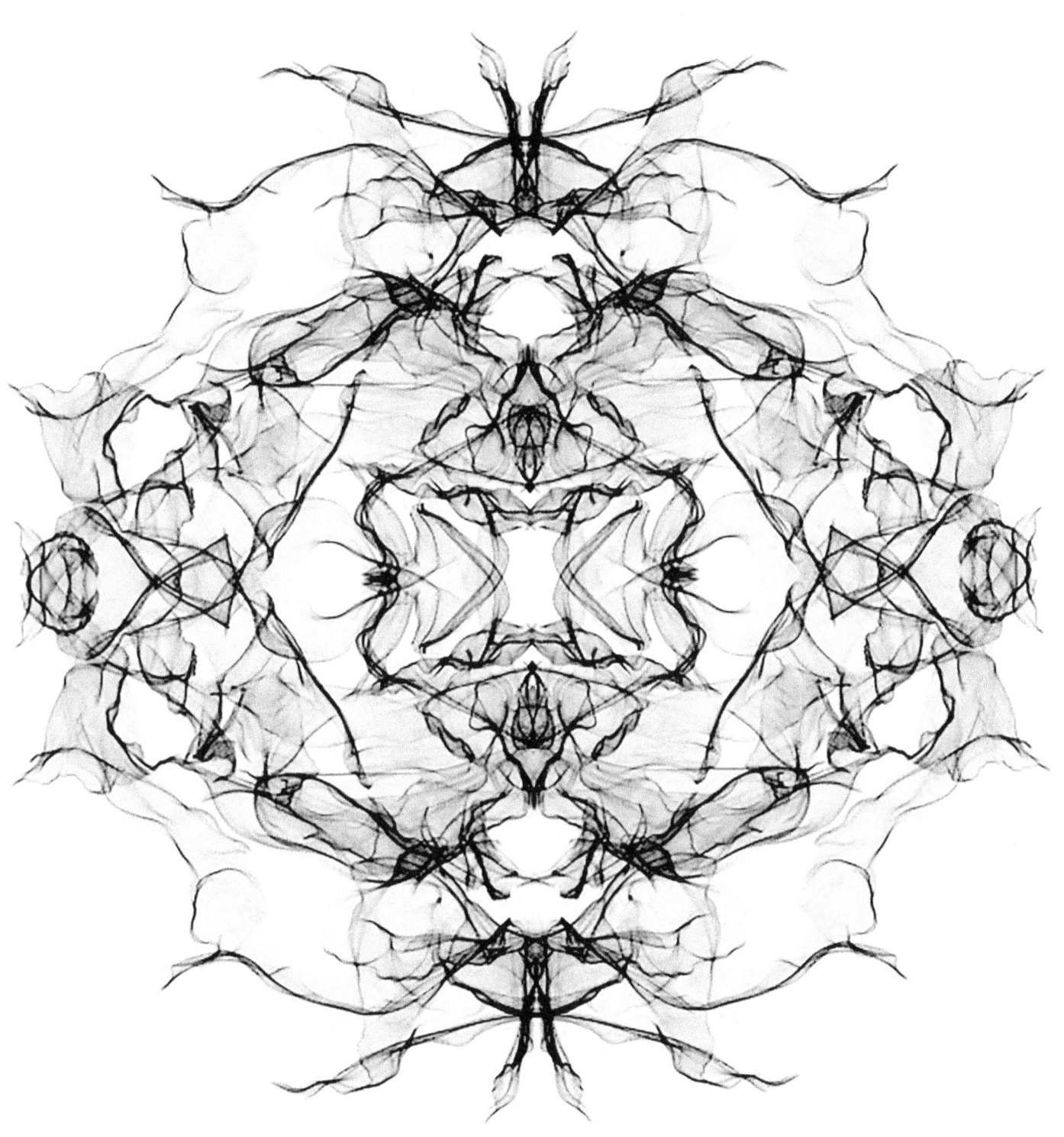

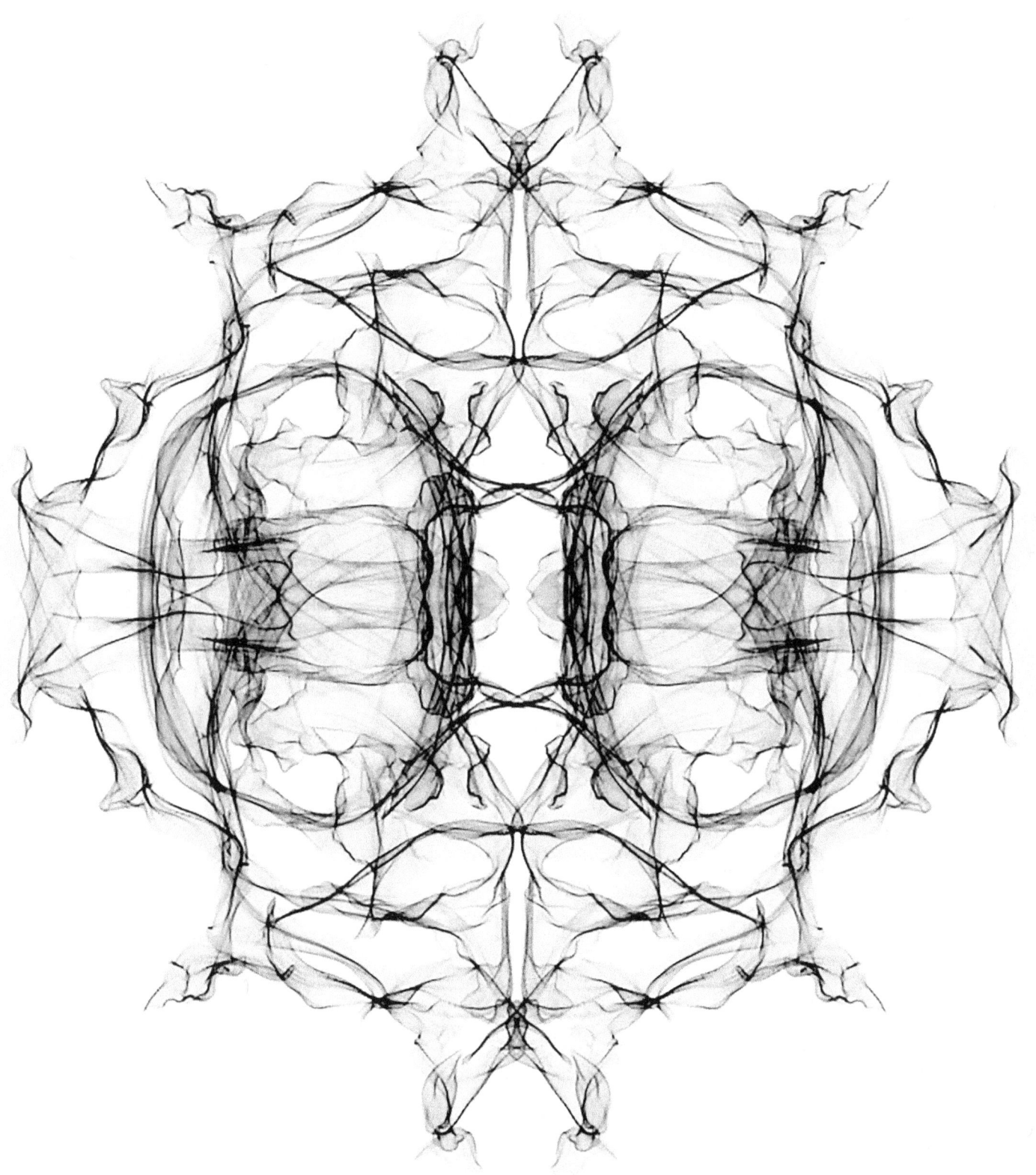

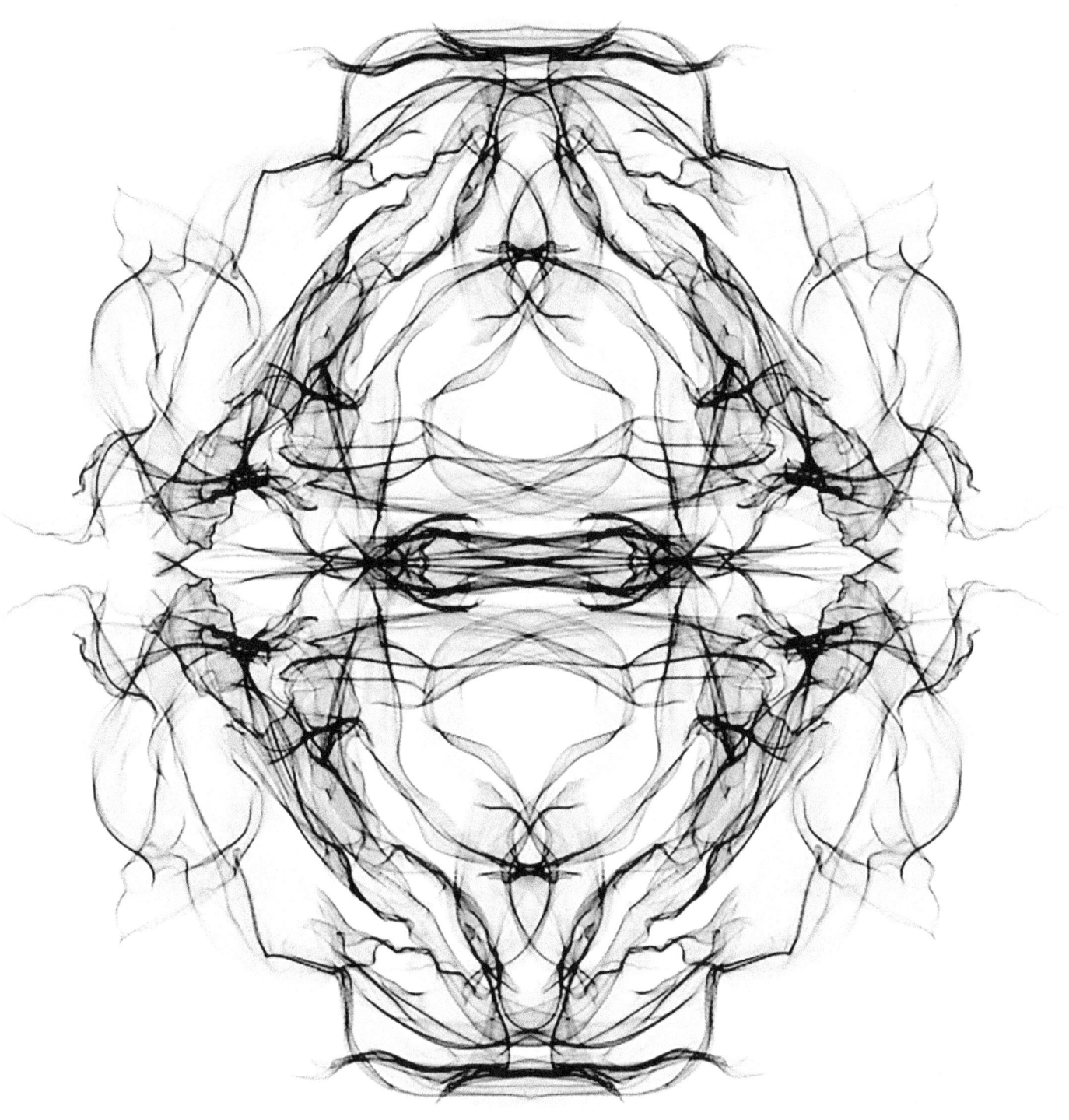

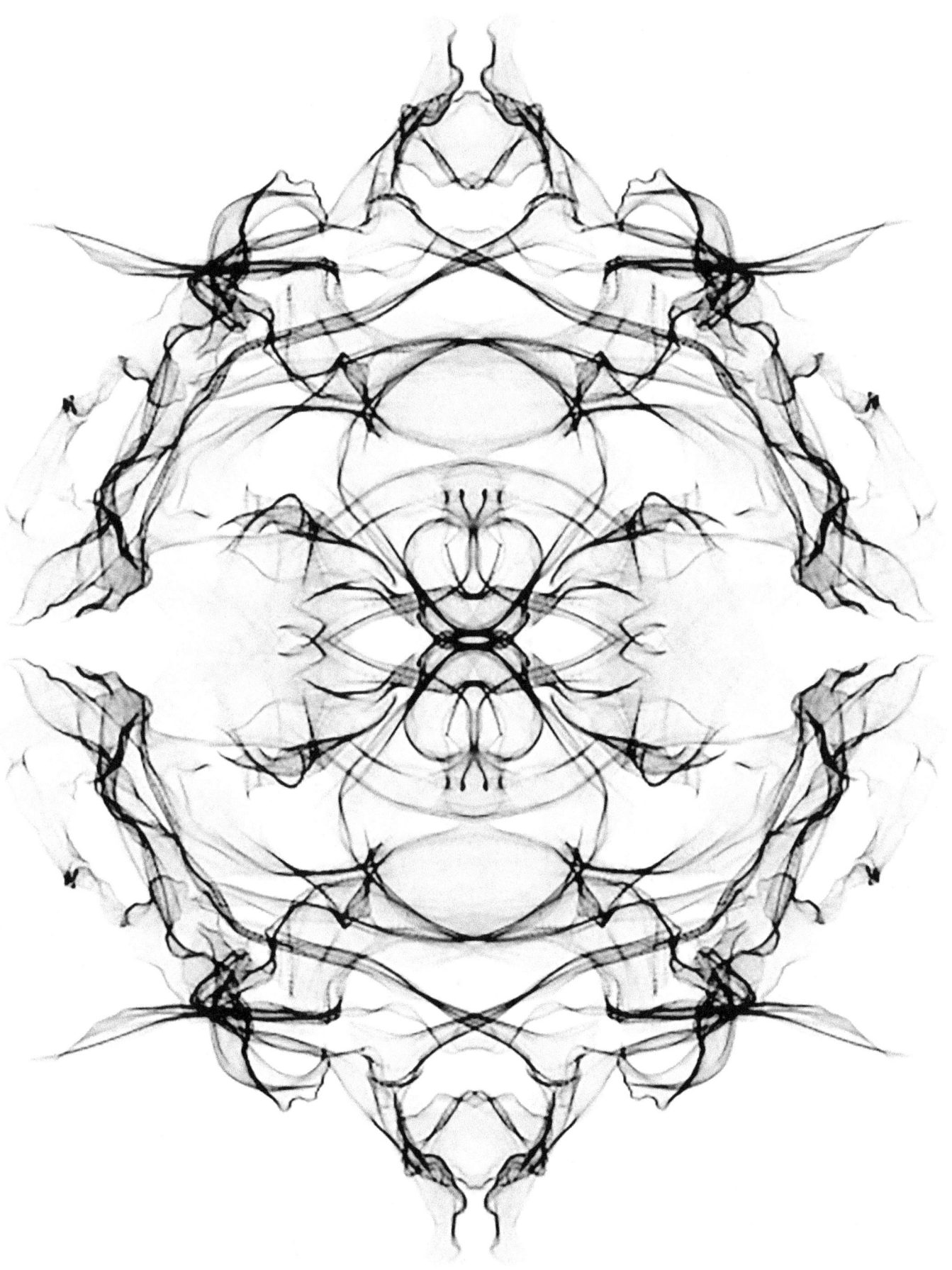

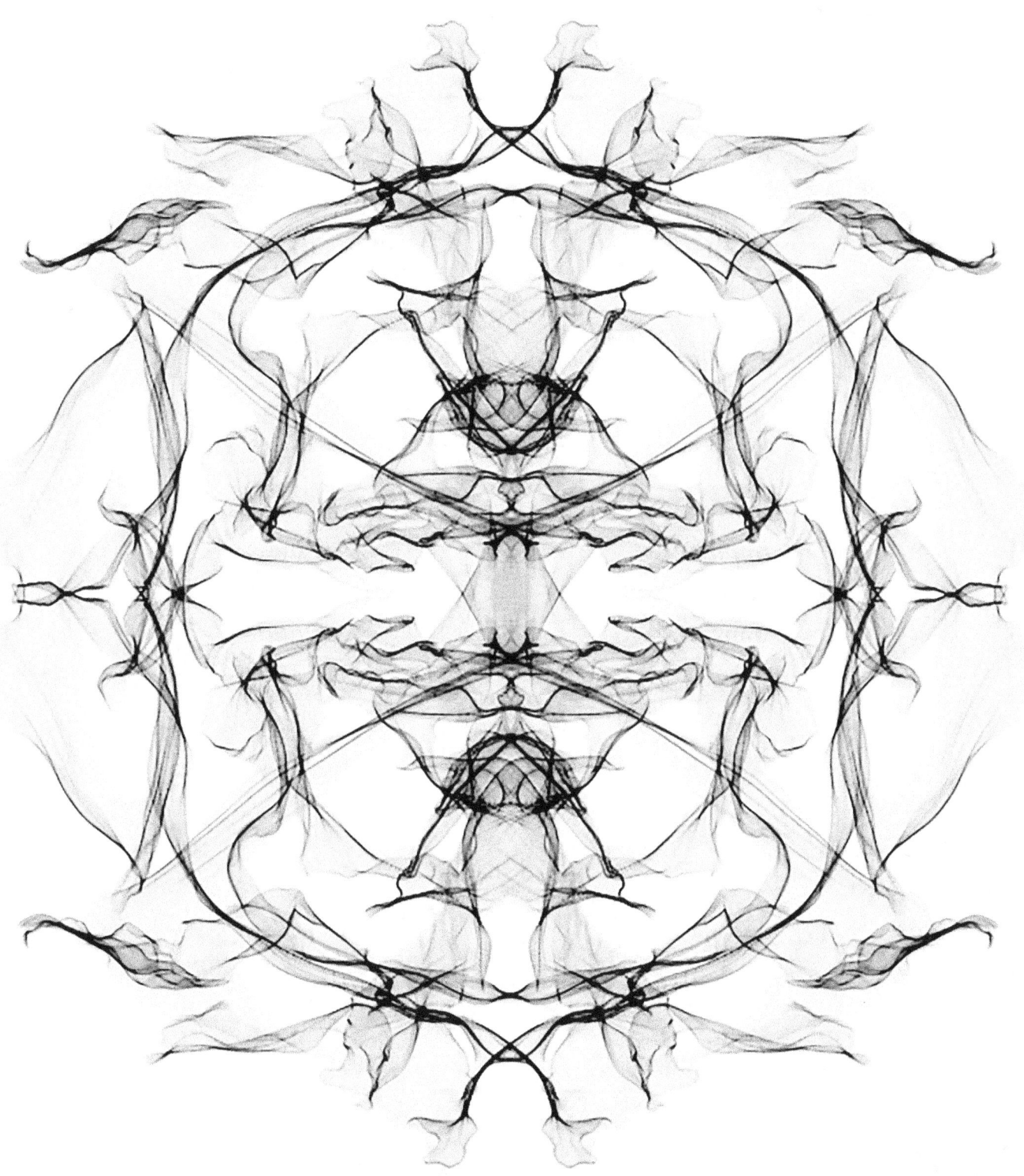

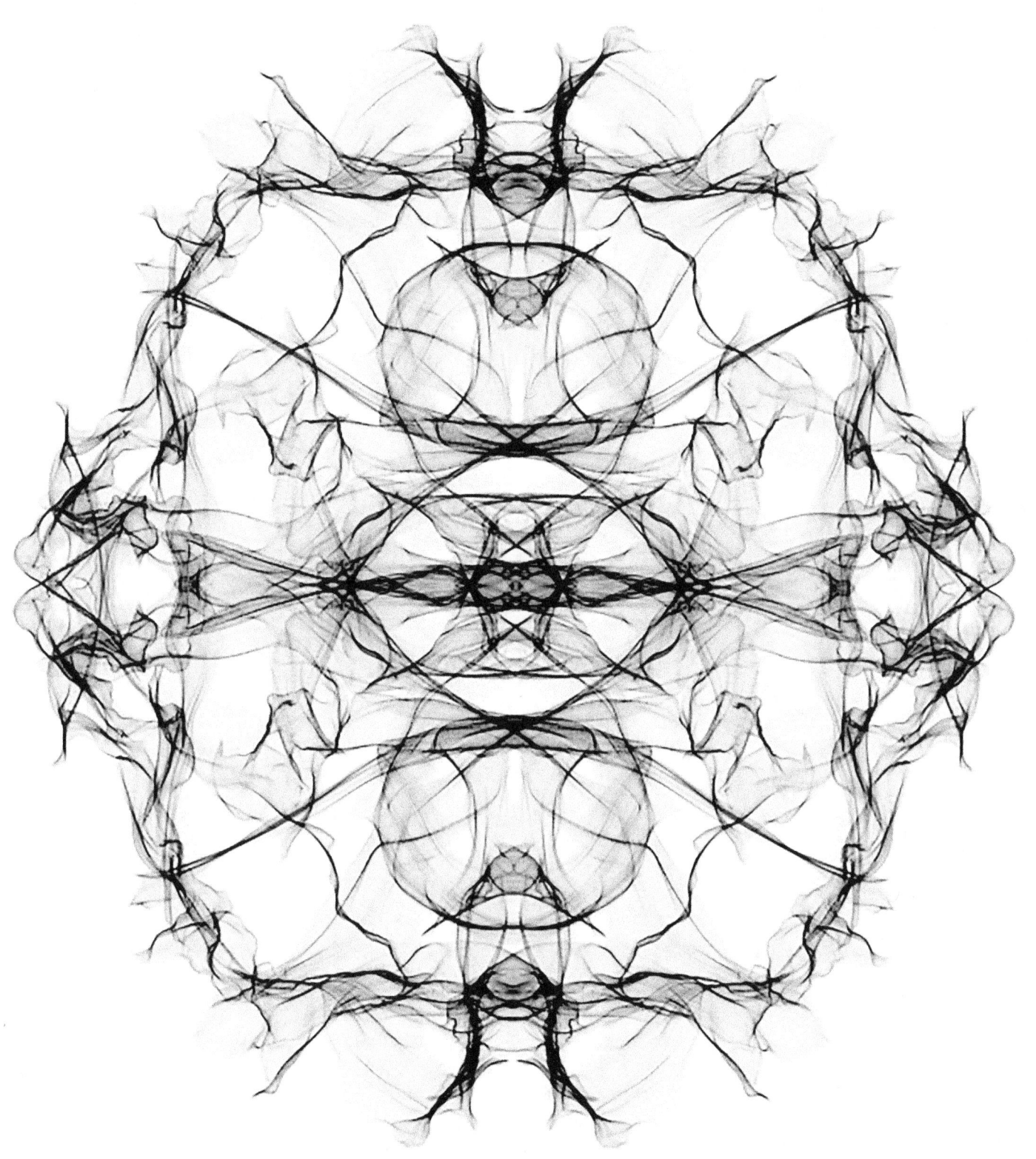

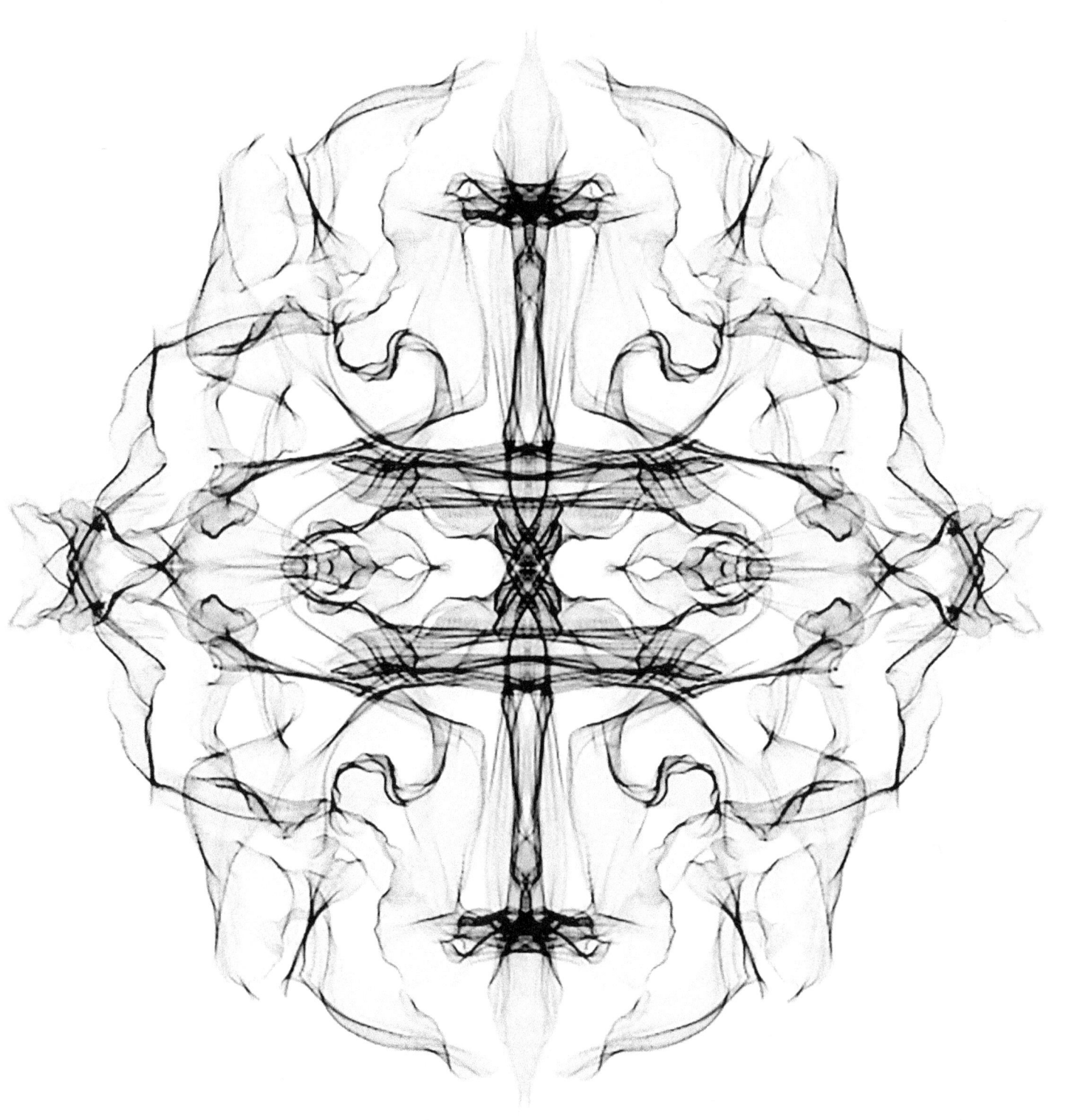

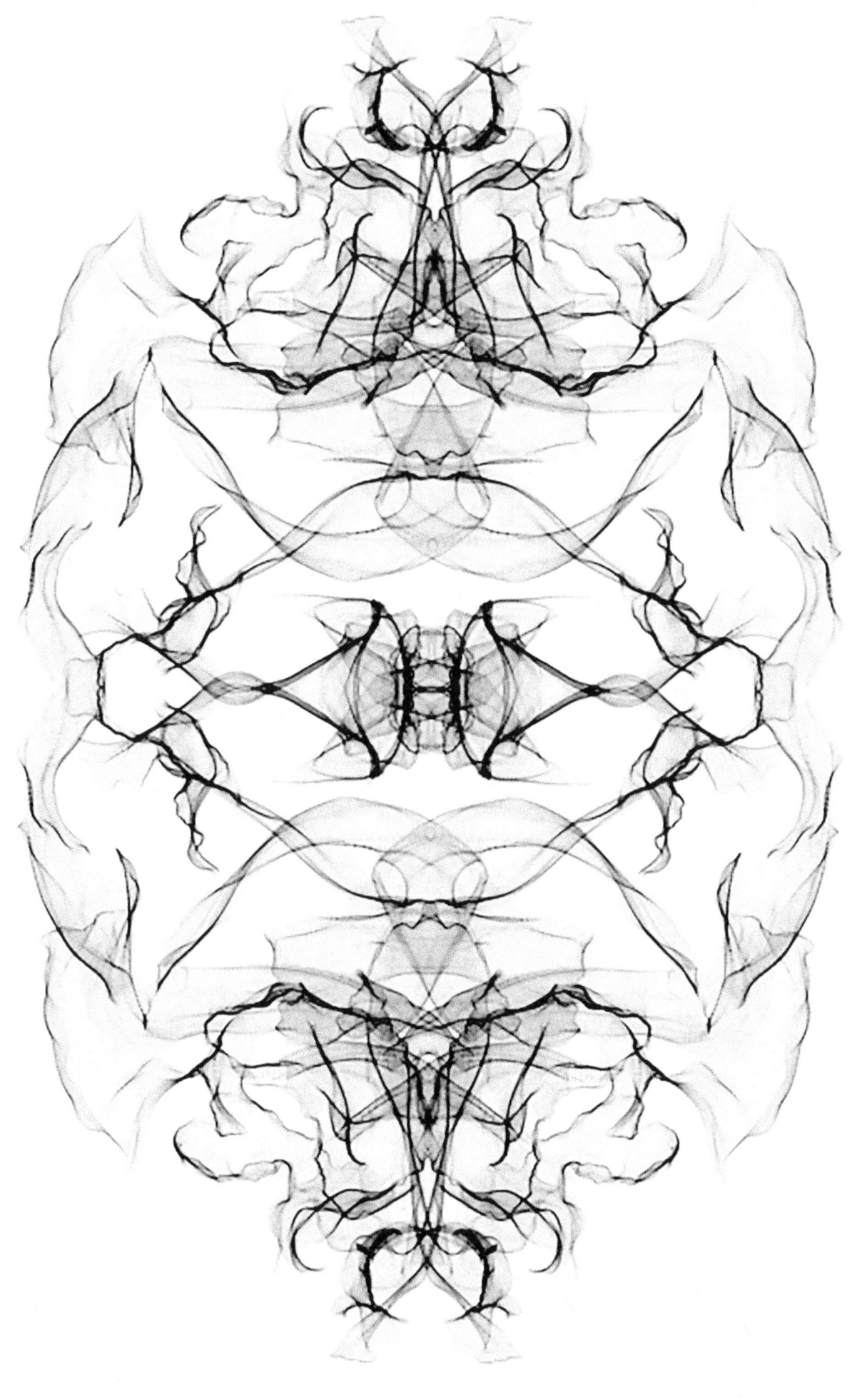

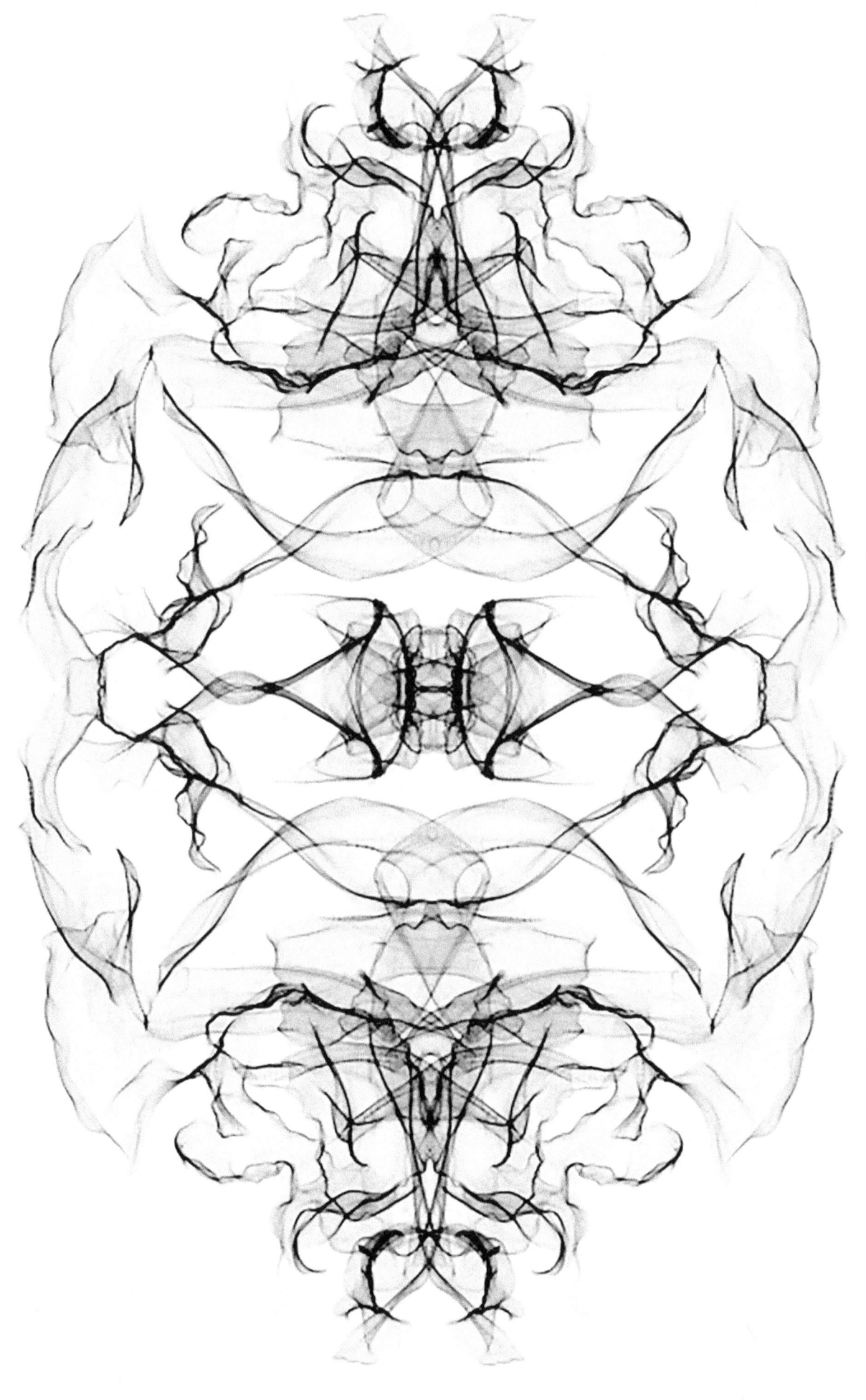

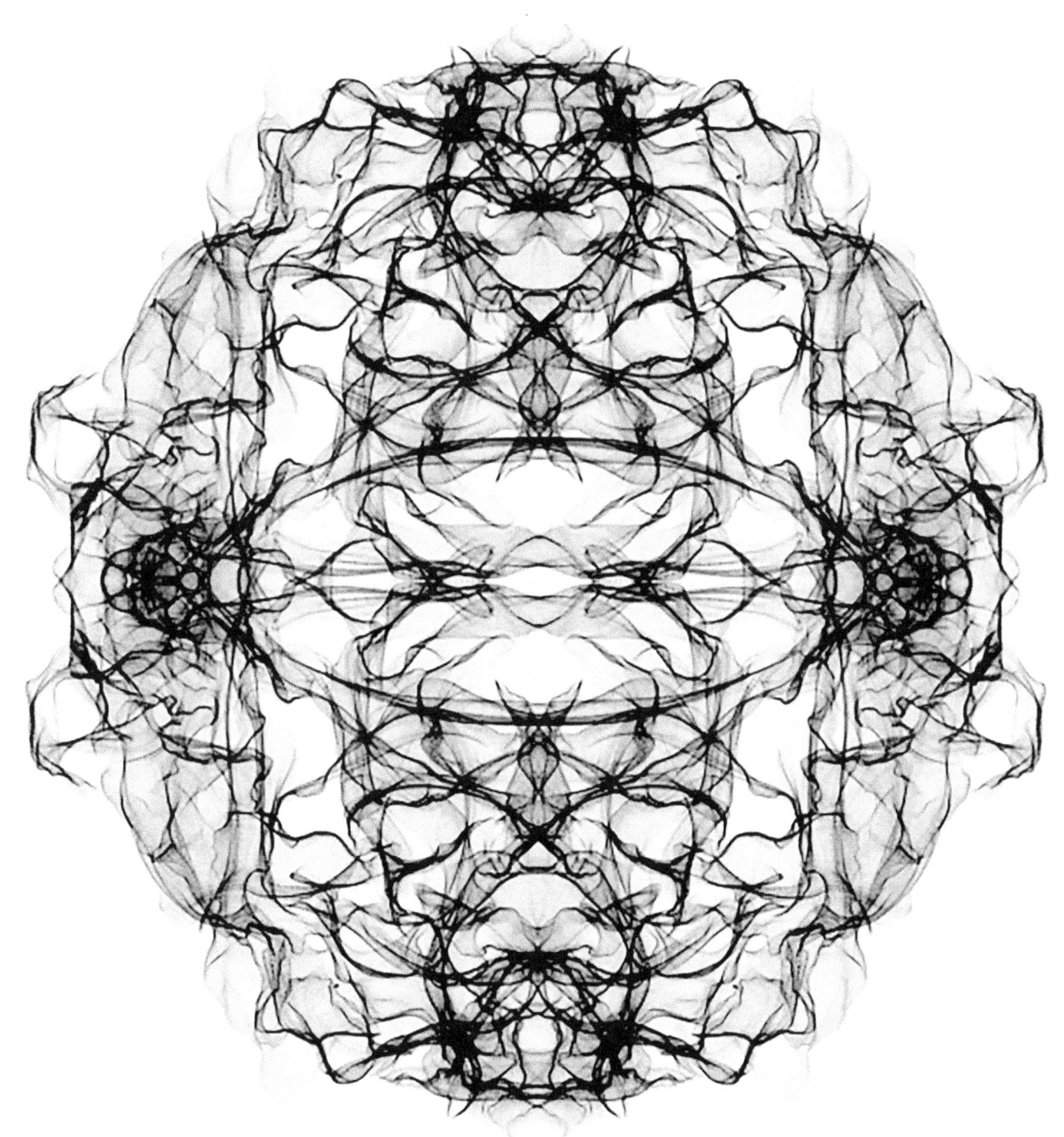

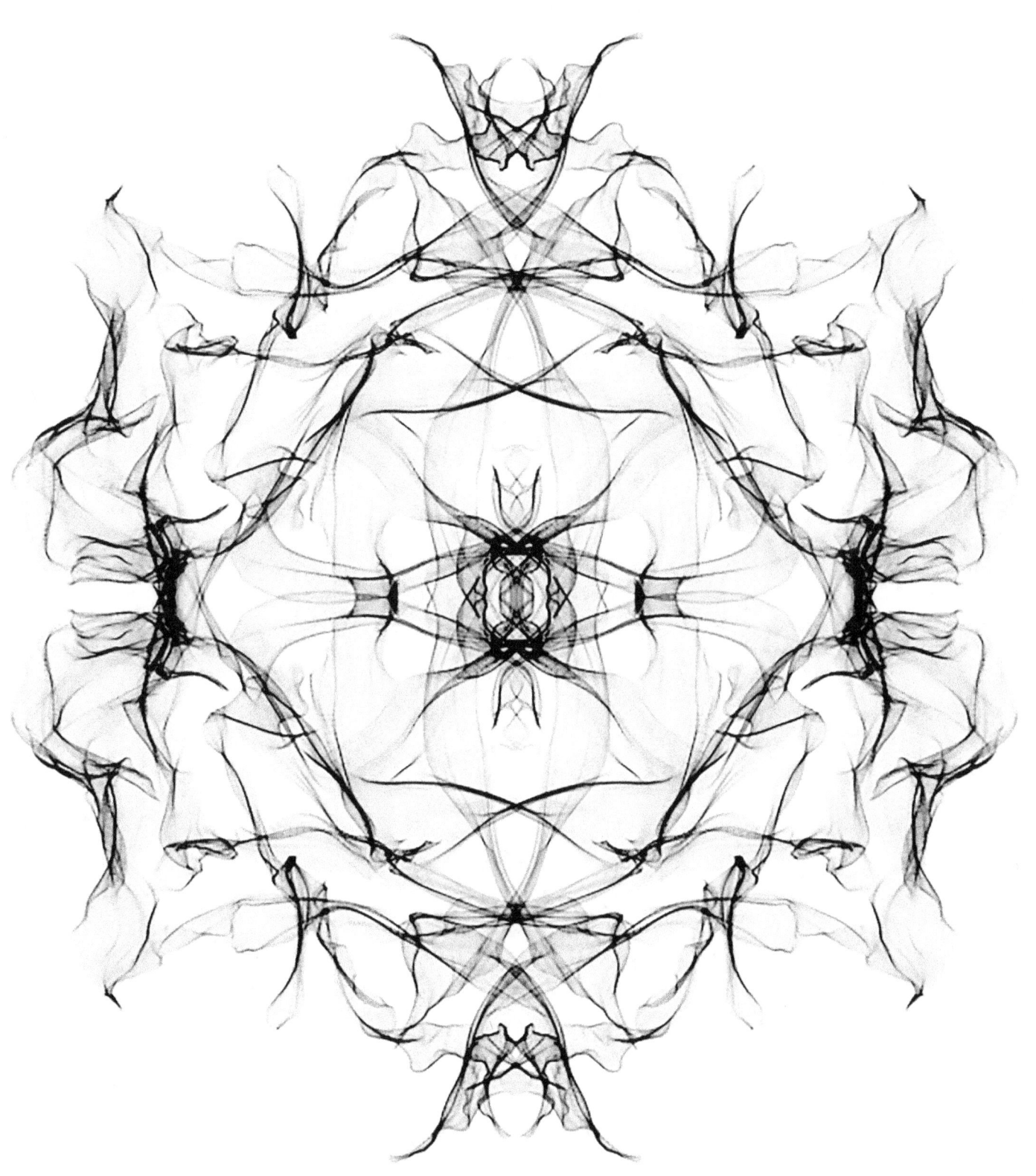

*Test a few of the Dark Side Designs from
Mephisto Coloring Therapy
Dark Side Volume 4*

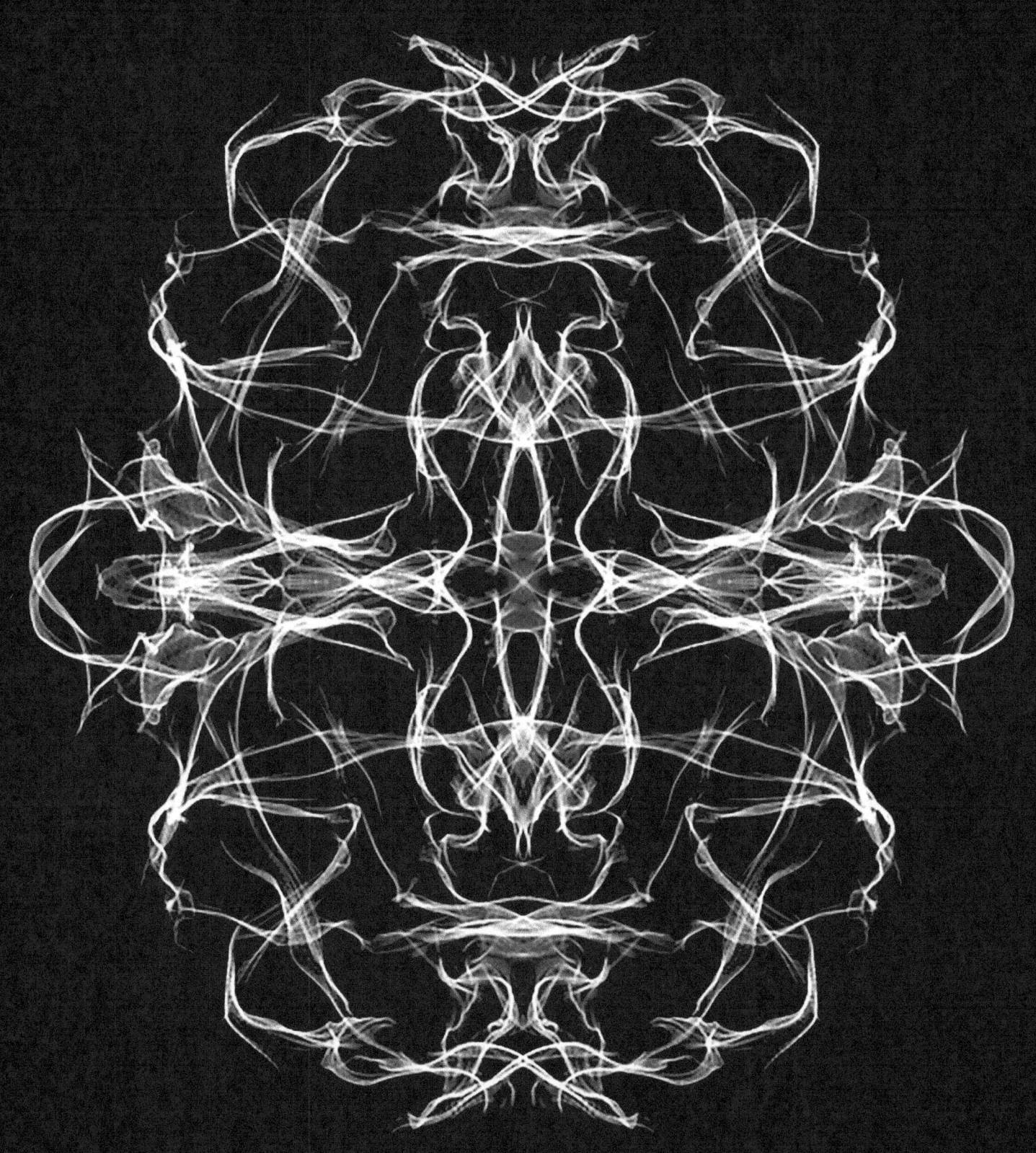

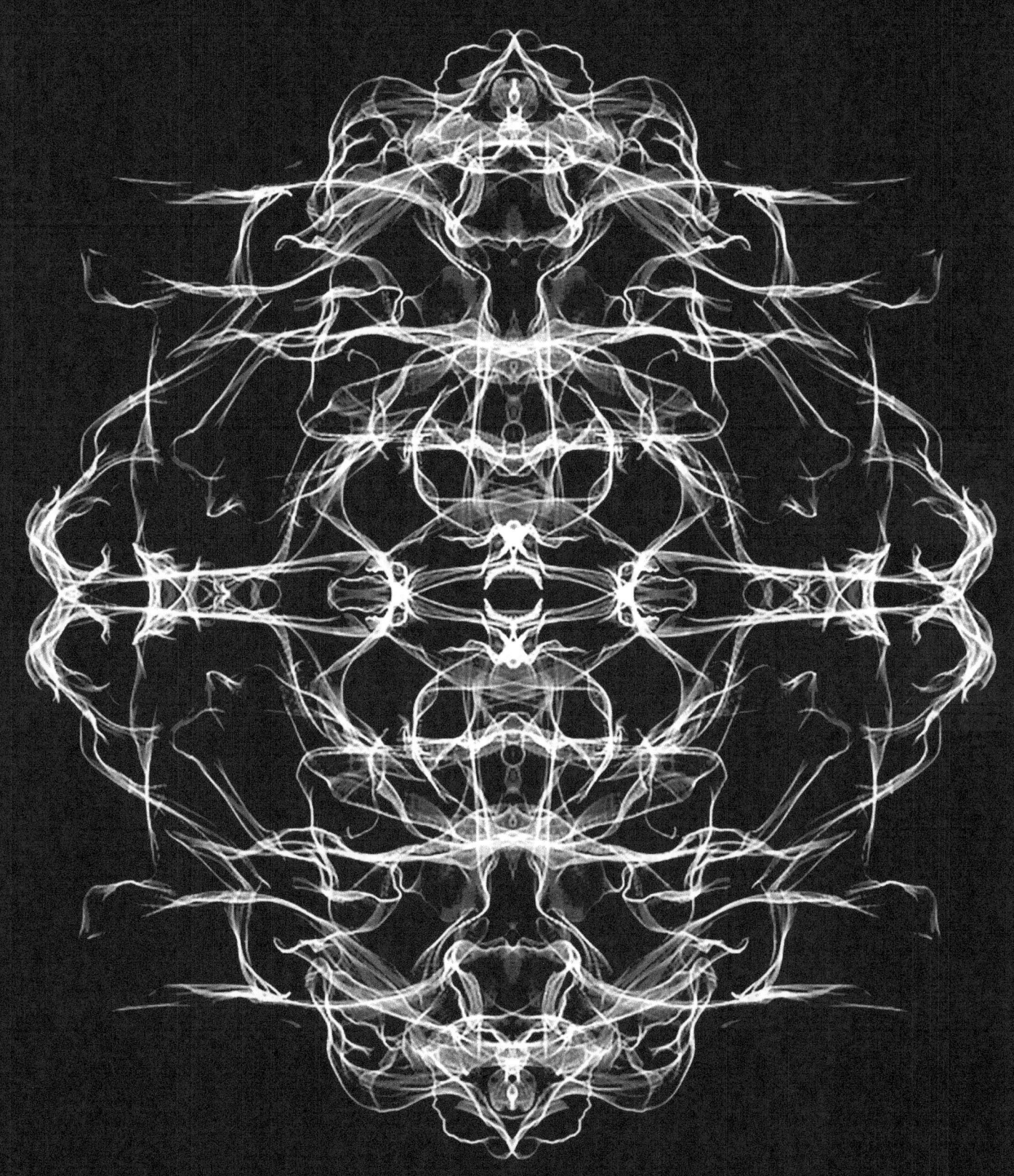